Graduates'
Guide
to
Business Success

**(Solutions that Enable College Graduates
to Excel in Business)**

**by
Emerson Taylor**

10 9 8 7 6 5 4 3 2 1

**LIBRARY OF CONGRESS CATALOG CARD
NUMBER: 96-86516**
Taylor, Emerson
Graduates' Guide To Business Success
Solutions that Enable College Graduates to Excel In
Business
Includes Index.

BOOK ORDERS: Additional copies of Graduates' Guide
to Business Success may be ordered from 800-247-6553,
24-hours a day by major credit card, mail order or check
from BookMasters, Inc., P.O. Box 2039, Mansfield, OH
44950 (FAX Orders 419-281-6883)

INTERNET INFORMATION AND ORDERS:
http//www.bookmasters.com/marktple/books/00160.htm
For a preview of Graduates' Guide to Business Success and
direct purchase (or fax) order information.
ISBN 1-888069-06-6 $14.95

Graduates'
Guide

to

Business Success

**(Solutions that Enable College Graduates
to Excel in Business)**

**by
Emerson Taylor**

To Cathie, whose support and encouragement made this book possible.

Acknowledgments

Special thanks to professional writer, Kate Winters, owner of Biography for Everyone, who put life into a businessman's factual draft and tapes: especially her constant requests for more "grad's experience" examples which greatly improved reader's understanding. Thanks to all the recent grads, human resource executives, business owners, and managers who read my drafts and provided their invaluable corrections, changes and opinions, especially Connie Colluci, Cherie Durand, Mike Greenhalgh, Fred Gillette, Bob Stock, Charles Sullivan, Kathy, Eric and Jill Weber, and Peggy Williamson.

Pronoun Footnote:

Instead of the cumbersome he/she or him/her, I have used he and him to represent both males and females in some chapters and she and her to represent both females and males in other chapters.

Table of Contents

Table of Contents (continued)

How This Book Benefits Graduates

While working as a campus recruiter twenty years ago, I began noticing the lack of understanding new grads had for what business required of their successful employees. Throughout my business career as I hired, managed and sometimes had to fire new graduates, I watched many of them struggle to learn their new duties and establish relationships. No real guidance or training was provided on how to adjust and fit in. No one gave these new grads any simple tips to help avoid mistakes and get promoted. Their adjustments, sometimes made painfully over five years, could have been made in five months had they only been given some basic guidelines.

I decided to someday write a book which would be a simple reference to help new grads speed up their learning process, avoid mistakes and succeed faster. It would also greatly benefit businesses, allowing their new grads to be more competent, confident, and productive, while at the same time decreasing the number of errors made.

Many mistakes grads make can be avoided. I've seen the same errors repeated over and over again. And so it is with this goal in mind that I've written this book which offers basic day-to-day, common sense solutions. For instance, it would be beneficial to grads to understand what business wants, expects and even demands. They don't realize how different the business world is from school, or how an inappropriate business appearance can harm them. Grads often discount their managers' opinions of them and the value of developing positive relationships, thinking it's only their achievements that guarantee success. As you read "Your Boss" it will be clear why no opinion is as important as the boss's. "Most Important

Skill" chapter will convince you of the importance of developing solid mutually beneficial relationships.

I've designed this book for grads who are entering business and who want to speed up their adjustment from (typically) five years to just a few months, resulting in a "fast start."

A "fast start" in today's business world is important for several reasons. First, a fast start signals a faster promotion and identifies a grad as having management potential. Second, if another grad gets the first promotion, he will likely be the first into management and ten years from now will be your boss.

A grad needs to understand the most common mistakes and how to avoid them. For instance, many grads enter business from a customer's point of view. After all, they've been a "customer" of their school environment for sixteen years. But they're no longer the buyer; now they're the seller. This simple understanding — and adjustment — makes all the difference between a grad perceived to have an "attitude" and one who is respectful, willing and helpful.

I've seen grads advance swiftly with a positive, "can do" attitude. That's the way I've written this book: positively, from a business point of view. Not that business is always right, but that's the point: those who are already successful within companies are those who are calling the shots. You would do well to understand their expectations and their rules.

I've always liked business. It's fun, it's challenging, it's rewarding. I hope to pass along that sense of challenge and fun to you.

This book is about being successful faster with fewer mistakes. If you've got to work you might as well enjoy it, make an impact, and be recognized and rewarded for it. That is what this book is all about!

Emerson Taylor

Chapter 1

DIFFERENCES BETWEEN SCHOOL AND BUSINESS

Quick Reference			
• Your Adjustment to Business			
• Differences Between:	School	vs.	Business
Achieving Success:	Individual	vs.	Teamwork
Critical Ability:	Tests	vs.	Relationships
Structure:	Quantified	vs.	Subjective
Grad's Role:	Customer	vs.	Employee
Performance:	Objective	vs.	Judgements
Communication:	Written	vs.	Verbal
Prestige:	Senior	vs.	Trainee
• What Grads Should Know			

To be successful in business the first things a grad should consider are the many differences between school and business and how to adjust to them. Your ability to adjust will make the difference between your success or failure and your enjoyment or disappointment in the business world. This chapter will present those differences — School vs. Business — and explain some of the new skills you must develop to make the quickest adjustment.

YOUR ADJUSTMENT TO BUSINESS

There are vast differences between school and business. There are differences in situations, your role in each situation and the skills necessary to be successful. When you compare your role as a student in school and your new role as an employee in business, almost every aspect of the situation is different. How well you understand these differences and how quickly you develop the new skills to succeed are the keys to making the successful adjustments from school to business. The following differences provide a basis for comparing previous situations in school to your new situations in business.

DIFFERENCES BETWEEN
SCHOOL AND BUSINESS

Achieving Success:
Individual vs. Teamwork

SCHOOL

In school you worked independently much of the time. You achieved success by attending lectures, reading books, writing papers and taking tests. You simply didn't have to rely on other people to do a good job. You could do it yourself and get the grade you deserved. If you did work with other people it was for a specific project, not for a final grade. Or, you may have studied with others, but the tests and grades were individual. In school a high percentage of your success was achieved individually.

BUSINESS

In business almost all of your success will be achieved based on cooperation with other people. You will be judged by what you and your manager, customers, department, or company achieve. Often your success will be determined by others you have no control over, like team members. In the first few years you will probably not have the most important role within any group. You will be expected to do your job, but your success will be determined to a great extent by what others accomplish. In business 90% of your success will be judged on the results of your cooperation with other people.

One adjustment necessary to achieve success is to recognize how much teamwork affects your success and to learn how to be a good team player. An entire chapter is devoted to teamwork and improving your team-playing abilities.

Critical Ability: Tests vs. Relationships

SCHOOL

In school the most critical ability was to understand books and lectures, then to take tests or to write papers on what you had learned. If you were very good at reading books and taking tests you would have received good grades and been successful as a student.

BUSINESS

In business the most critical ability is to develop positive relationships. If people like you, respect you, and want to help you, you will have a great advantage in accomplishing your goals. Your ability to influence, motivate and get cooperation from all types of people is the critical ability that will determine your success in business. That's what Ann found out in her first job, early enough to make a necessary adjustment and learn to value relationships.

Ann had always been an excellent student, graduating with a 3.85 in accounting. Basically shy, she was proud of her ability to concentrate, study, and consistently be on the Dean's List. After graduation Ann landed a great job in the internal audit department of a large multi-national corporation. During her first few months of work she became very frustrated that the other employees working on her audit team never let her do her job without interference. They seemed to spend too much time discussing what was to be done. Ann turned to Meg, who had encouraged her to take the position months before.

Meg had graduated a year earlier and had recommended Ann for the job. An average student, Meg hadn't the discipline to get A's. She had spent time with friends in various clubs and organizations instead of studying all the time. Over a glass of wine after a harrowing week, Ann told Meg of her frustration. Meg spoke candidly with Ann: "I spoke with your audit team leader. He suggested that you might not be getting along with team members. Ann, working at this company I've found I have to constantly work with people having different ideas and motivations. How well I fit in and work with all of them will determine how well I do."

Ann defended her stance: "But I want to see the project through myself." Meg understood that Ann's frame of reference was based on school, tests and individual accomplishment. She needed to adjust to a business and relationship frame of mind. "You're smart, Ann. No doubt about that, but in business you succeed by using what you know to get things done. You get things done by getting people to agree with you and then work together to achieve common goals. I want to share something with you, Ann. It won't be common knowledge until next week that I'm being moved to another audit team as team leader.

I've found that getting people to accomplish common objectives has been my most successful ability. My boss has been helping me and he says the higher up I go — the more people that work for me — the less "hands-on work" I'll be able to do myself. It just gets to be more and more important to achieve goals through others."

Structure: Quantified vs. Subjective

SCHOOL
Schools are intentionally quantified, that is, they are designed to measure an individual student's knowledge. To do this they require a highly structured, compartmentalized grading system to measure students' knowledge of a subject. Each class is quantified by how many points it takes to achieve an A, B, or C. Every class is given a number of credits; the requirements of each degree are spelled out by the number of credits needed in each department. All these classes, grades, credits and degree requirements are made known to the students when they first enter school. To be successful a student chooses a degree program and follows the class and credit requirements. The student always knows exactly where he is in the process and how much it will take to finish. Students, therefore, become accustomed to this highly structured, quantified system.

BUSINESS
Business is much more subjective (than objective or quantified), in the same way your personal life relationships are subjective. As an example, how many percentage points or credits does it take to determine if a friend likes you (or if her parents like you)? Business is much less structured because it consists of

relationships between people, their opinions of you, and how much they believe or trust you.

Business is also subjective because it is open-ended. Your first promotion may come in six months or six years; your career could be over in three years or in thirty years. The path to success is also open-ended. One successful CEO may spend ten years in sales and ten years in finance while the next may have spent twenty years in production. There are no set requirements to achieve success.

Many grads have difficulty adjusting to the lack of quantified structure in business as compared to school. A part of the grad's success in business will be the ability to adjust to teamwork, learn the importance of relationships, and acknowledge the subjective nature of business.

After Ann had been working in the audit department for a year and a half she became frustrated with not knowing how she was doing. She'd taken Meg's advice, concentrating on developing positive relationships with other employees on her audit team. She called Meg, who had been promoted to another office. "Meg, I'm really concerned that I'm not making any progress toward a promotion. I like my job, it sure beats those long hours studying in the library, but I don't feel like I'm getting ahead. I'm just not getting the feedback I need to know how I'm doing."

"Welcome to the business world, Ann," said Meg. "We were spoiled in school with the constant feedback from papers and tests and grades. It's annual reviews in the world of business, Ann. You'll be lucky if your manager does your annual performance review on time."

"So how do I deal with the frustration, and how do I know how I'm doing?" Ann asked.

Meg continued, "It's natural to feel frustrated because things don't seem to happen as fast as they did in school, but the good news is that business is a lot more fun than school.

Just relax and concentrate on doing a good job and developing your relationships. Promotions will come to you, I promise. Anyway, I hear you're doing great." Meg was right, too. Ann would be offered a promotion before her next performance evaluation.

Grad's Role: Customer vs. Employee

SCHOOL
As a student you were a "customer" of your school. You or your parents paid money for the service your school provided: an education. The school was designed to help you learn and your educational success was the object of the school. Adjustments you may have made were directed toward the goal of getting the most benefit from the dollars you paid to the school.

Employees of the school worked at the school for a paycheck and a chance for a career. If they didn't do their jobs they were replaced.

BUSINESS
Instead of being a customer within your new career in business, you will change to the role of employee. Instead of you paying money to receive services, the company will pay you money to perform a service for them. Inherent with this change comes your new responsibility to make all the adjustments that a successful employee needs to make. You must get to work on time, do your job and make whatever personal adjustments are necessary. Many grads make the mistake of not realizing this change in roles. They think their company's primary concern is to enhance their careers and help them succeed. The company will help you succeed to the degree that you help it succeed.

As an employee of your new company it is your job to serve the customers of that company and to help the company make a profit.

Performance: Objective vs. Judgements

SCHOOL
In school the highly quantified grading system is objective and impersonal. Many grades are determined by written tests requiring specific textbook-based answers, given to all students at the same time. The grading system is explained at the beginning of the class, with personal judgements limited to term papers and projects which make up a small percentage of the grade. Also, your "annual performance rating" or overall GPA consists of grades given by several instructors over the course of two or three semesters or quarters. You could have a total of ten or fifteen different people evaluating you on separate criteria. This diversity greatly reduces the effect of any one person's judgement and decreases the importance of personal relationships.

BUSINESS
Performance in business is evaluated subjectively and often by the opinion of one person, much the same way you have been evaluated in your personal life. If you ever tried out for a sports team or a band you know it was one person — the coach or band leader — who made a judgement on your performance. If you had a summer job you got a pay raise because your boss thought you did a good job. In business your performance will be evaluated at least annually by one person — your manager or boss. The decision will be made on overall job performance without tests or percentages. This reliance on one person's judgement for your entire annual performance rating puts added emphasis on your ability to develop positive relationships.

The grads who adjust early to the importance of the employee-manager relationship (whether they like their bosses or not) will be more successful. The best way to make a successful adjustment will be explained in "Your Boss," chapter 6.

Communication: Written vs. Verbal

SCHOOL
In school a great deal of the information you learn is written. You read text books, lab manuals and reference books for research papers. Much of what you learn is achieved through reading; the remainder is spent listening to lectures with very little one-on-one discussion. The information you produce to get your grades (to have your performance judged) is even more heavily written. Most of your performance is judged on written tests and papers with little, if any, verbal evaluation. Verbal discussions are typically short and limited to comments in class, or personal discussions with friends or students who tend to be your same age and of a similar background.

BUSINESS
Conversely, in business 80% of the communication you give and receive consists of one-on-one or small group interaction. Discussions with all ages and types of people with whom you may have little in common is the rule rather than the exception. In discussions you'll be expected to explain your ideas and defend your beliefs, disagreeing without offending, while changing others' opinions. At the same time, it's equally important to understand the beliefs and opinions of the different types of people with whom you'll come in contact. Your success will be determined by how well you use the words that motivate people and how well you avoid the words that offend them.

Examples are scattered throughout this book, especially in "Most Important Skill," "Politics," "Communications" and "Making Mistakes Positive." To many grads who have spent sixteen-plus years relying on their reading and writing skills, the conversion to verbal expression can be a difficult adjustment.

Prestige: Senior vs. Trainee

SCHOOL
As a college senior your prestige was obvious when compared to the lowly freshmen. But beyond even that, you were at the top of the sixteen-plus year process of education. Everyone was impressed with what you had achieved. You were considered one of the elite: highly educated, a future leader of our country. Your potential and possibilities were limitless: president of a company or President of the United States.

BUSINESS
When you start your first job you will drop from a position of high prestige that you held as a college senior to one of very low prestige. You are now a graduate or management-trainee. As a trainee you will know less about your job, your company, its products and customers than any other employee. Even employees who didn't finish high school will know more about their jobs and the company; at least they've been around awhile. Besides, most employees will be older than you and will be more experienced in life and business in general. It may be difficult to accept, but you are starting out at the bottom of your new company.

One of the most difficult adjustments grads must make is accepting this change from being a senior at the top to being a trainee at the bottom. As one grad put it, "During your senior year you're on top of the world. When you start working everyone is higher than you are. The only thing lower is whale dung because it's at the bottom of the ocean." You must mentally adjust from being on top to being on the bottom. . . from being at the end of the educational system to being at the beginning of your new career. Just think how many possibilities lie ahead!

What Grads Should Know:

YOUR ADJUSTMENT TO BUSINESS
  *How well you understand the difference between school and business and how quickly you adjust will determine how successful you are in business.

DIFFERENCES BETWEEN SCHOOL AND BUSINESS
  *Achieving Success: Individual vs. Teamwork
    In school 90% of your success is achieved as an individual; in business 90% is determined by co-operation with other people.

  *Critical Ability: Tests vs. Relationships
    In school the most critical ability is taking tests and writing papers; in business it is establishing positive relationships that motivate people.

  *Structure: Quantified vs. Subjective
    School is quantified to measure individual knowledge; business, like your personal life, depends on subjective opinions.

*Your Role: Customer vs. Employee
   In school you were a paying customer; in
   business you are paid to adjust and produce.

*Performance: Objective vs. Judgements
   In school tests are designed to be objective; in
   business personal judgements determine success.

*Communication: Written vs. Verbal
   In school most is written; in business 80% is
   verbal.

*Prestige: Senior vs. Trainee
   In school a senior is on top; in business you start
   out at the bottom and must learn to show respect
   to everyone.

Chapter 2

MOST
IMPORTANT
SKILL

Quick Reference

- The Most Important Skill
- How To Develop It
    Learn to "Read People"
    Create Positive Relationships
    Use Positive Relationships to Achieve Your Goals
- What Grads Should Know

The most important skill you'll ever employ — in business and out — is to "read people" and use the knowledge you gain to motivate them in accomplishing your goals. This chapter shows you how to develop those positive relationships that will allow you to achieve your goals.

THE MOST IMPORTANT SKILL

The most important skill anyone in business can develop is the ability to create positive relationships with people of all types and all ages, and to use those relationships to achieve goals.

As we discussed in chapter one, what creates success in school and what creates success on the job are different. What were the most important skills in school? Attending lectures, reading books and passing tests can get you through school even if you have "zero" verbal skills. Your verbal skills — what you say — is not an important skill.

Contrary to school, the most important skill in business is based on what comes out of your mouth and how it comes out — your verbal skill in creating positive relationships. Some graduates have wasted their careers, never figuring it out, lost somewhere on the road map to success. They were passed over for promotions they could have had and frustrated by a skill they never learned. The great news is that it is a skill that can be learned and developed. Understanding the importance of this skill and practicing it will give you the ability to succeed.

You can practice creating positive relationships in any group setting: military, church, business or family. Of all the skills in business, this one is not just "The Most Important Skill," but it is the one you will use the most if you are to become successful. It is also the skill that will become more and more important as you climb higher up the corporate ladder.

HOW TO DEVELOP IT

You develop your most important skill by practicing and using its three parts: 1) learn to "read people," 2) create a positive relationship with others, and 3) use those relationships to help you achieve your goals.

1) Learn To "Read People"

First, become a people watcher. Observe very carefully the actions, moods and motivations of others. Second, become a people predictor. Try to predict others' behavior in various circumstances. Evaluate your prediction. Try again.

Everyone uses this skill of "reading people" daily — successfully or not — often unconsciously. I can share the "refinements" necessary that will help ensure your success.

Practice is the most important part of developing this skill. Make it a game you play every day. Observe others by watching them carefully as they interact with co-workers, friends and family; in good moods and bad moods; under stress and when relaxed. Be a good listener to the people you study. Spend twice as much time listening as you do talking. Listen to your boss. Listen to others in meetings, listen when you must interview another. Be an active listener. Ask "why" in order to understand another's motivations.

Predict what you think they're going to do. Observe their actions. Were you right? If not, revise your prediction and try again. Try until you get it right. People are different, so be prepared to "refine" your abilities in developing this skill, as did Kevin, a young graduate who worked for a low-key, shy boss.

Now Bob, Kevin's boss, appeared calm and composed. He entered Kevin's cubicle one morning, handing him a file folder of information, "I want you to get on this." Kevin took the folder, smiled and said, "I'm just wrapping up the Jason project. I'll get right on it." He didn't ask when his boss's project was needed. The Jason project snagged, delaying Kevin, and he was unprepared for Bob when he walked in at 4:45 that evening.

"Have you got that ready for me yet?" Bob asked. Kevin felt a knot in his stomach, "No, the Jason project was trouble, but I'm finished with it. I'll work on it now." Bob turned on his heel and without a word left the office. Kevin felt stunned.

John, a co-worker hired eighteen months previously, overheard, "I've been working for Bob for a year and a half. You've got to learn to read him; when he brings you anything it's got to be the highest priority. Otherwise, he never would walk it in here himself." Kevin felt defensive, "So why didn't he tell me it was so important?" John responded, "You've got to learn to read him. That's as strong as he gets."

People are different. They behave and are motivated differently. Once you learn to observe and predict those with whom you work with some accuracy, you'll be ready to establish a positive relationship with them.

2) Create Positive Relationships:

Next, create the positive relationship which will allow you to achieve your goals. Find out what people want and help them get it. If you try to help them and can't, be sure they know that you tried. Back to Kevin and Bob . . . .

The next week Bob and Kevin were on their way to a meeting. Kevin asked Bob if there were any projects with which he needed help. "I'm having trouble getting those employee pamphlets printed. I don't know what the problem is but they've got to be out by Friday." When he got back to his office, Kevin started checking into the pamphlets. He learned that the print shop's schedule called for a six-day wait time, not three days as Bob required. Kevin also found out the printer was having problems with a priority job because he couldn't get time on the computer. Kevin went to Bob and asked if his department could free up time on their computers so the printer could complete his priority project, thereby making time for the pamphlets. The printer used Bob's department computers, finished his priority job and was then able to print the pamphlets by Friday. Kevin delivered them to Bob two hours before the deadline.

Kevin had been able to create positive relationships with both Bob and the printer by finding what both needed and helping them get it. Because he understood Bob's low-key management style, he'd been careful to ask questions until he could pinpoint exactly when the pamphlets had to be completed.

Kevin made a special point of thanking the printer for completing the pamphlets. He wanted to make sure the printer realized it was Kevin who had arranged to use Bob's computers, so he asked if the priority job had turned out OK. It had. The printer appreciated Kevin's help. That was an important step. Be sure others are aware of what you do, or what you attempt to do for them. They'll be more willing to help you when you need something done in the future.

POSITIVE PERSONAL RELATIONSHIPS: Don't restrict positive relationships to business. They can also be established in personal non-business situations. Be especially alert to people's interests and hobbies. Very valuable, positive relationships can be built from shared interests. Remembering that Bob had a reputation for being very quiet, shy and withdrawn, Kevin additionally found out that Bob only relaxed and opened up when he talked about his favorite hobby, training dogs. In fact, Bob had pictures of dogs all over his office.

One day Kevin mentioned to Bob that he was considering buying a dog. He asked for recommendations on what type of dog to consider and where he might start looking. The change in Bob was amazing to Kevin. He brought books from home for Kevin to read and initiated conversations at Kevin's cubicle after work to discuss which breeds had which traits. "The most important part of choosing a dog is to get one that compliments your personality," Bob told him. Later that month he went with Kevin to help him pick out a golden lab puppy from a litter sired by his 109-pound male.

By accident Kevin had learned a valuable lesson in developing positive relationships. Find out what people want — or are interested in — whether it's job related or personal. You can capitalize on developing these mutual interests and achieving mutual goals.

3) Use Positive Relationships to Achieve Your Goals

Once you establish these relationships, never abuse them. You'll want to be aware of another's: 1) position, 2) what they can and can not do, 3) relationships with others, and 4) legalities and ethics of the situation.

Do not ask anyone to do anything in conflict with their best interests. Ask others to do things that will serve their interests and needs. Most people will want to help you if they can. Try to find areas where you both can win. Ask others to do only what they have the ability to do.

When you have a situation where a positive relationship can help you achieve your goals, make sure you consider not only your goal but continuing the relationship.

It was less than a month later when Kevin needed updated instruction manuals printed for a training class. Time was short — the class was coming in the following week. He knew the printer was swamped and it would be a huge favor to ask him to print the manuals before his other scheduled work. Kevin walked downstairs to the print shop to talk to Ed. "We've got the machines going late every night trying to keep up with the printing around here," Ed told him, dark circles beginning to show under his eyes. Kevin had second thoughts about asking him to put the manuals at the top of the schedule. Ed continued, "Tell you what, though, if you can get help down here for three nights we can get them done for you and still stay on schedule."

Kevin hated to give up his evenings, but he also knew how important the manuals were for the training class. What were his options? He could tell Bob, his manager, about the problem, but Bob would only go to Ed's manager, forcing them into overtime. He didn't want Ed mad; their relationship was both positive and important. He wanted the manuals printed, but damaging the relationship was not the way to do it. Kevin decided to personally help Ed after work.

Kevin learned a lot about printing in those three nights; it really was interesting and the manuals looked great. As Kevin turned to leave, Ed called him over to his desk and handed him a copy of the Manager's Report which was just being printed. "Thanks for all the help. Maybe this can do you some good if you put it in the right place." Kevin knew exactly what he meant and gave the Manager's Report to Bob. Bob was grateful to get the report early, "This is great, Kevin. It will give me a big

*advantage in preparing for the manager's meeting. Whatever
you do, don't lose that relationship you have with Ed."*

   *Kevin reflected as he returned to his office: The relationship
with Ed had really paid off, especially now that he'd been able
to give his boss an advantage over the other managers. Kevin
knew his decision not to ask Ed to do his manuals out of order
was a good one. That would not have been in Ed's best interests.
Kevin had done the extra work necessary to strengthen the
relationship with Ed. That relationship had ultimately paid off
with the advance report which further strengthened his
relationship with Bob. Kevin had been right in hesitating to
use his relationship with Ed to ask for a favor until he could be
sure Ed would also benefit as a result.*

   Carefully protecting relationships until there can be a win/
win situation is definitely the best practice. Positive
relationships, after all, take time to create. They're so valuable
that they're worth protecting.

What Grads Should Know:

THE MOST IMPORTANT SKILL

   *The most important skill in business is to create
     positive relationships and use them to achieve
     your goals.

HOW TO DEVELOP YOUR "MOST IMPORTANT
SKILL"
   *Learn to "read people"
     - watch what people do
     - listen to what they say
     - learn to predict their actions

*Create positive relationships
- read people to find out what they want or like
- help them get what they want
- be aware of personal hobbies and interests

*Use positive relationships to achieve your goals
- ask for others' help
- ask for only ethical, honest help
- never abuse relationships
- find a common course of action that achieves your goals and benefits them as well
- thank others for helping you, or for trying to help

Chapter 3

GOOD WORK HABITS

Quick Reference:

- Competition: Be the Best
- Honesty and Integrity
- Work Hours
- Attendance/Absences
- Timeliness
- Neatness
- Workloads
- Break and Lunch Opportunities
- Perception is Reality
- Getting Your Money's Worth
- What Grads Should Know

Good work habits are easy to understand; like diets and budgets they're difficult to stick to. Habits form the basics of showing you are a capable, concerned employee. It's a mind set. But only knowing what to do counts for nothing; it's the doing that counts.

Everyone develops habits. Will yours work for you or against you? Understanding what work habits are expected of you is the purpose of this chapter. Then it's up to you to discipline yourself to follow through and to become the best employee.

COMPETITION : BE THE BEST

You're competing for more than being the best. You're also competing for assignments and relationships. You want to stand out for being the best at whatever you decide to do. You are in competition with more than your peers. You're in competition with other co-workers who have been there longer and are more knowledgeable about your company. You may also be competing with outside consultants, commonly called outsourcing.

If you do a good job with everything you're given, you'll be given the better and more important projects. The better job you do, the more sophisticated your assignments will become, the more likely you'll be recognized as being the best.

In school, your instructors probably gave out more than one "A." In business there may very well be only one "A." You will experience constant competition throughout your career for promotions and assignments. The first requirement is to always give it your best, as Chuck learned from his extra efforts designing a marketing video for his jewelry company.

OPPORTUNITY TO BE THE BEST:*Completing his first year in a jewelry company, Chuck heard about a new product line, Graduation Jewelry. He asked his boss if he could be involved in training for the new product. His boss said that the video to be used for the sales and trade show training was to be decided in three months at a senior manager's meeting. Two outside consulting companies and the sales department were making bids for the training videos and manuals. Chuck's department, the training department, hadn't bid. Chuck volunteered to prepare a video,written with the customer's perspective in mind,* *if his boss would permit use of their own video employees' expertise. Working nights and weekends he and the video team developed the script. The senior managers accepted it, with minor revisions, and applauded his efforts which saved the company $30,000. Chuck learned a lot about scripts and videos, but more importantly he gained in 1) strengthened positive personal relationships and 2) product knowledge. As a result of his efforts he was acknowledged for making his boss look good to senior managers, and he stood out as their company's specialist in graduation jewelry.*

HONESTY AND INTEGRITY

Reputation is extremely important. You'll be building your reputation the first few years you're on the job and maintaining it after that. Use every situation involving ethics and integrity to build a reputation for the highest level of honesty. Your reputation will follow you wherever you go.

Being Squeaky Clean

The best recommendation I can give is to be "squeaky clean." What is squeaky clean? It's demonstrating honesty in everything you say and do. It's very important to initiate and maintain the standards for which you want to be known. How do you go about making your reputation for being squeaky clean?

One of the easiest ways is to describe what it is not. And what is it NOT is a progressive dishonesty which begins with small stuff and escalates to what eventually becomes noticeable. As an example, an employee might start taking a pen home, then perhaps paper clips. You can use the pen at home; it's no big deal. The next step might be a minor expense account item. You take the subway for $1.50 but you put down $7.00 for a cab. The rationale is that you're making up for something you forgot to include in the expense account you submitted last month. After all, it's not really stealing from the company, it's just being smart, right? The next step might be a small gift someone offers you, which you accept. Then there might be a petty cash fund — it might be all right to borrow a little out of it, after all it's an emergency, isn't it? Pretty soon you're stealing big stuff....

Don't do it. It isn't worth it. It's not worth losing your integrity; your reputation within the business community; your friends and your family; even your job. Some say it doesn't matter, that you won't get caught. Even if the people around you are stealing and you are aware of it, don't even be tempted. Be squeaky clean.

Stealing Time

Let me give you another example of stealing. Your company is paying you for your time. Taking time away from work when you aren't working — yet getting paid — is stealing. Using company resources is another area of stealing: copier, telephone calls, the postage meter. Don't be tempted to make personal copies for yourself, your family or your friends; inexpensive and convenient copy shops have proliferated within the past decade, cost little and are fast. Telephone calls can easily be checked. It's not simply a matter of the call which is billed to the company — that's money out of the corporate coffers — but it's a matter of the time you took by being "off-line" and unproductive.

Demonstrating Integrity

Expense accounts can be an excellent place to demonstrate your integrity if you're honest. If your travel expenses are $1.50, note $1.50. Be proprietary; spend the company's money like you'd spend your own. Aim at being frugal without being stingy. This will help you build your reputation in managing resources, people and departments. The company will regard you with approval as they see you develop money management skills, stay within budget and be conscientious about spending company money.

Entertainment and lunch appointments are two other excellent opportunities to develop your reputation for being squeaky clean. If, at a business lunch, someone else picks up the tab — whether from your company or from another — don't be tempted to turn in a receipt to pad your expense account. Demonstrate your honesty to yourself and to those around you. The payoff of developing a reputation for honesty and integrity will reward you much more than any short-term gain. Guaranteed.

What's Expected of You?

There tends to be huge differences between what students expect and what companies expect of business people when it comes to honesty. Whereas in college it might have been cool to steal a sign for your room — and even joke about it later — business finds this entirely inappropriate. Business judges by a very different set of standards. Business is not tolerant of "minor" theft.

Keeping Confidences

Another opportunity to display your honesty is in the need for discretion. Keeping confidences. If someone tells you not to tell something, don't tell. If someone of authority asks you something you've been asked not to tell, you might say: "Sir, I've been asked not to say anything." Appeal to their need to maintain discretion. "If you asked me not to say something, I wouldn't say anything, honoring the trust you placed in me. I feel very uncomfortable. I've given my word. I know you don't break your promises and I know you don't want me to break mine." Use this uncomfortable situation to make a statement of your integrity and to build your reputation.

WORK HOURS

Expect to work long hours during your first six months, perhaps the entire first year. There is no way around it, but there are three very good reasons for it. First you not only have 1) a job to do, but 2) you have much to learn about your job, the company, and other employees, and 3) relationships to develop, using your most important skill (see chapter 2). I'm not sure one of these is any more important than the other. Certainly developing relationships is every bit as important as doing a good job. Learning what to do and how to do it is paramount to doing it. Expect long hours.

Adjust your work hours around your boss and the other people in your department. If your boss comes in early, by all means go in early. If your boss stays late, you'll do well to learn to adjust your work hours to staying late. There are three very good reasons to adjust your hours around the schedules of others. First, it's productive. It's a good time to do your work with people around who can help you when you have questions. This can be a most effective time. Second, you'll want to use that time to familiarize yourself with the things you don't have time to learn during the day as you're concentrating on mastering your job, like gaining a greater understanding about your department and your boss. Third, there's a social aspect to coming in early or staying late. Before or after work hours people tend to be much more receptive to chat, to give you information. During work hours there are demands on everyone's time. When quitting time comes, they might kick back and be more inclined to talk with you about issues that affect them — or that might affect you — that aren't specifically job-related. It generally will be easier for you to build personal relationships during this time. Chuck's unexpected conversation with Susan as he worked late one night earned him a great deal of help — help he could not have "asked for."

During one of Chuck's late evening sessions with the video employees, Susan, the manager of Advertising, happened by the open door of the conference room. "You must be working on something very important; I've seen you here three nights in a row and here it is 8:00 tonight." Chuck explained about the training video. Susan responded, "Maybe one of my writers would be able to help you; I'll check tomorrow."

The professional writer was a huge help. Later, during the senior managers' meeting, Susan was the first to speak in favor of the training video. Months later, after their work was applauded and approved, Chuck and the video employees laughed about how the whole project probably succeeded because of that one chance after-hours discussion that got them professional help on the script and the first vote in the senior managers' meeting.

ATTENDANCE/ABSENCES

Attendance is vitally important to your reputation. Do everything you can to avoid absenteeism. Not being at work when you could be is stealing value from your company. If you are not totally incapacitated, don't stay away from work. If you are absent due to sickness or accident, read your company's manuals and learn the rules regarding absences; then abide by them. Many large companies require that doctor's forms be completed after a designated number of days off the job.

Sunny Day Absences

Never, never give any company the idea that you stayed home because it was a sunny day. Don't jeopardize your own chance of promotion. This is a major difference from school where absenteeism is not only tolerated, but occasionally condoned. There is much less flexibility and freedom in business as far as time off is concerned.

It is common for companies to employ computer programs which track reoccurring absences. Those who take Fridays off in order to enjoy a longer weekend — or those who have a rough weekend and use Monday to recover — are warned about absenteeism. Their reputations will suffer. Be sure this is not you.

Long Absences (More Than A Couple Of Days)

Long absences of several days or weeks are occasionally unavoidable. If it is possible to do any part of your job, by all means make arrangements to have work sent home. Answer what calls you can from your home phone. This shows a good attitude, that you're a conscientious employee who wants to contribute and who is willing to extend extra effort. Again, remember that you're in competition with everyone else. If you aren't at the job site representing yourself, practicing your most important skill, developing positive relationships and looking good, someone else will be. Missing work is not only expensive to the company, but it's expensive to you.

TIMELINESS

Although it's important to be on time for appointments and meetings, it's absolutely critical to be on time — or early — for deadlines. Time is an issue which is much more critical in business than it was in school. Be a person who is aware of time. In school you can get away with being five or ten minutes late. In business, being prompt will help you earn the reputation for punctuality which you'll need as your success grows. In business there is never a good reason to be late, always a reason to be punctual and occasionally a reason to be early.

Deadlines

Deadlines are where timeliness is critical. I've seen graduates who work very hard on a project, making it a masterpiece rather than getting it out on time. They don't understand the importance of deadlines.

Always be on time or early for deadlines. Because everything in business is interrelated, timeliness is crucial. Deadlines in school are often relative. You might make up a test, take an incomplete, or drop a class. That is not the way of business. In business many people are working on the same project and depending on your part in order to complete theirs.

Different parts of the project must be completed before other parts can be started.

Meetings

Arrive five minutes early at every meeting you attend. Use that time to get to know the others, especially those you don't work with on a regular basis. Meetings often cross departmental or divisional lines. Those five minutes before meetings can be time well spent practicing your most important skill, developing personal, positive relationships.

Appointments

Being prompt for appointments is imperative. It's not a good idea, however, to be early for appointments as it is for meetings. Successful business people tend to be very exacting with their schedules. Their calendars are planned around their appointment times. You should arrive a few minutes early, walk around, identify where you'll meet, but not go in. Announce yourself at the exact time of your appointment.

Chuck made a habit of always arriving seven to ten minutes early for every sales meeting. Before the sales training meeting started, he'd overheard two trade show employees talking about the new product development before plans had been announced. He'd prepared an informal presentation for his boss by the following day. Although he made a point of being early to each department meeting, he arrived precisely at 9:00 for the appointment with his boss.

NEATNESS

There are advantages to looking neat. Many managers often equate neatness with being organized, on time and effective. If you're not already neat, you can practice neatness which will help you become organized.

If you dress neatly and have an orderly briefcase, desk and office, it will appear you are well organized. You may be the kind of person who has papers piled all over the top of your desk and files stacked beside it. You may be able to locate everything within seconds, but the impression you give is that you are disorganized.

Those perceived as organized will often get the assignments which are more challenging, larger and more complicated. These are the projects you want.

WORKLOADS

This section addresses enthusiasm and willingness to work, how to handle too little or too much work, and who you report to in conflicting or dual-reporting situations.

Too Much Work

Develop a willing and eager attitude with regard to workloads. Be in an upbeat mood, smile, be friendly. Create a reputation as a hard worker who is always looking for things to do. Become known as the one who does the best job they can, who works as quickly as possible and then returns for more. Guard against appearing to be a complainer or a whiner, especially when you have much to do. If you don't think you can finish on time, return to your boss and ask for help to prioritize tasks. This sends two messages. First it identifies what you understand to be a priority and reassures him that you are attacking the most important assignments first. Second, it makes your boss aware of how much work you are tackling. If you are required to work late or come in early, you want to have your boss know so you'll get "credit" for the extra effort.

Too Little Work

Conversely, if you run out of work this will be your opportunity to show your willingness and enthusiasm. Instead of dragging out a two-hour job into a four-hour job get on with it and then ask for more. Offer to help others with their projects.

Special Projects

Additionally, volunteer for projects. Special projects can give you recognition not only from your boss, but from other managers. Special projects often cross divisional lines, like the United Way Fund or other charitable organizations. Exposure: that's the benefit of volunteering for special projects. Additional exposure gives you a chance to start new positive relationships.

Work assignments should always be given to you by your boss. If a work assignment comes from anyone else, check with your boss to make sure it is acceptable for you to work on that project versus the one your boss thinks you're working on. It is your boss's responsibility to schedule your workload so the most critical tasks are completed first. He may authorize someone else to supervise you on a particular project and allow them to determine your workload. But be sure your boss is aware of your work assignments so you aren't spending time doing something of lesser importance, neglecting what is crucial.

Chuck remembered his excitement after receiving approval to produce the script for the graduation jewelry video. He knew he didn't have enough time to handle all facets of the project, but with video employees' help, he felt confident he could present a first-rate production. Two weeks into actual production, however, he felt overwhelmed. The video employees suggested he ask his boss's opinion on getting an experienced project manager to help him organize and monitor the whole project. He wanted all the credit, but reluctantly he told his boss about his dilemma. "Glad you asked for help," he said, "This is a big project and you'll need help to get it done. I've asked Jack to cover two days a week for you. That will give you the time you need for the project. Good luck. You're making this department look good; we're all here for you."

Over-Promising

Guard against over-promising. Underestimating what you have to do can get you into trouble. You don't want to indicate something will take you a day when it takes a week, or a week when it takes a month. Even though you may have worked hard, it will reflect poorly on you if you consistently disappoint other people by not having your work completed as promised. Make sure you understand a project before you start. Know how to judge not only what your part will be in completing it, but the approximate amount of time it will take you to finish it. If you don't understand what is required of you, or how much time you will have to complete a project, talk with others about it.

BREAKS AND LUNCH OPPORTUNITIES

The three key words guiding you to make best use of breaks and lunches are 1) opportunity, 2) customs and 3) reputation.

Opportunity

First, breaks and lunches provide the very best opportunity to acquire information about your company, your job, and others within your organization.   Build positive relationships by finding out what's going on within the company, within your department and with other people. Ask about their projects, their challenges, their interests. Never miss an opportunity to break or lunch with others. Be the opposite of reclusive. Try to take breaks and have lunch with as many different people as possible, unless it's the custom of your department or your boss not to do so.

Customs

Second, you will be expected to adjust to the customs of your department. As you learn to fit into your working group you'll become a part of your departmental culture. If your working group has a custom of eating together, eat with them. If everyone goes to lunch together on Fridays, go to lunch with them on Fridays.

Reputation

Third, develop a reputation for being the person who takes the shortest lunches and the shortest breaks. You want to give others the impression you are eager and willing to work on the projects given you. If you sit down first when the group does, get up and leave with the first person.

PERCEPTION IS REALITY

We've alluded to perception being reality many times. It's crucial to understand that people's impressions of your work are just as important as the work you do. Perception has everything to do with how well your boss "thinks" you are doing. Your responsibility is to give your boss and other key people the opportunity to see you as eager and willing. Allow them to see you coming in early and/or staying late. If those key people stay late, you stay late. If they come in early, you come in early. Make sure your boss knows you're putting in extra hours so you get credit for extra work.

Perception is reality. Maintain a busy image: keep busy, look busy. You may be a person who is accomplishing much, but may not look as though you are. Be conscious of "the image of work." As an example I would cite Hal, one of our best employees.

While Hal was thinking he used to lean way back in his chair, put his hands behind his head, and stare at the ceiling. To anyone walking by it appeared as if he had nothing to do. One day a senior manager entered my office asking about Hal. I explained he was both creative and a good producer. "He looks like he's doing nothing," he said as he left. I stopped by Hal's office later that afternoon and suggested he keep a pencil in his hand and try to get in the habit of staring at his desk as he was thinking. Sometimes it's just an image — he just looked like he wasn't doing anything. So, look industrious; it's not dishonest, it's just image. Allow those in management to always perceive you as busy.

GETTING YOUR MONEY'S WORTH

When you purchase a stereo to listen to or a car to drive, or hire a plumber to help you fix the sink, you want your money's worth. Your company is no different; they're paying you to get a job done.

It's no more than what you'd ask of someone else if they were working for you in your own company. You'd want them to show up, be on time, do their best, be honest, keep deadlines, be organized and communicate workload information. What your mother told you holds true. Minimum is not satisfactory. Adequate is not good enough. Put yourself in your company's shoes. They simply want to get their money's worth from you. To really be successful in your career, "the best" is what you'll need to be.

What Grads Should Know:

COMPETITION: BE THE BEST
   *You are in competition with other grads and
      employees to get your next promotion.

HONESTY AND INTEGRITY
   *Your new company expects a higher degree of
      honesty than was expected in school. Be
      "squeaky clean" and avoid any type of dishon-
      esty.

WORK HOURS
   *Expect to put in long hours the first year because
      you really have two jobs: being productive on

your job and learning about your company, products and people.

ATTENDANCE/ABSENCES
*Avoid absenteeism, especially the Monday or Friday pattern.

TIMELINESS
*Deadlines: be on time or early for all work assigned to you
*Meetings: be five minutes early and use time to get to know people.
*Appointments: never early, never late; always be on time.

NEATNESS
*Management equates neatness with being organized and precise; make sure your work, desk or cube and appearance are neat.

WORKLOADS
*Too much work — ask your manager to give you the priorities
*Too little work — finish quickly and ask for more
*Special projects - volunteer for them and do your best
*Temptation to over-promise - be careful to avoid this.

BREAKS AND LUNCH OPPORTUNITIES
*Use breaks and lunches to meet and get to know co-workers, fit into your department or company's customs . Always leave with the person who takes the shortest lunch or break.

PERCEPTION IS REALITY
*Never underestimate people's opinions of you; their opinions can be just as important as your actual accomplishments.

GETTING YOUR MONEY'S WORTH
*Make sure your company gets its money's worth from you; adequate is not enough. You must try to be the best.

Chapter 4

NEW SKILLS

```
Quick Reference:

 • Organization
 • Calendar
 • Filing Systems
 • Lists
 • Criticism: Accepted and Given
 • Compliments and Acknowledgements
 • What Grads Should Know
```

New skills are important business talents that you must develop to become successful. These skills are more complex and harder to achieve than good work habits. They are also very different than the skills required to be a good student. The skills required to be the best in business are going to be developed and refined throughout your entire business career. In fact, the higher up you go, the more important these skills will be to you.

ORGANIZATION

In business the volume of work, along with the diversity of projects and changing priorities, make it impossible to remember where you need to be each hour of the day and what you should be doing. The need to develop organizational skills is critical to guarantee you meet all project deadlines, schedules and appointments. The three most useful tools to do this are calendars, files and lists. A calendar will keep your schedule of appointments and deadlines. A filing system will help you quickly find everything you need. Lists will keep you on top of every responsibility, deadline, project appointment and meeting.

The first step in becoming organized is to develop good organizational habits. Standardize what you do and when you do it. Set up a pattern of accomplishing certain tasks at the same time of the day, same time of the week, same time of the month. For example, set up tomorrow's "To Do" list each evening before you go home. On Fridays, before leaving the office, mark your calendar with those projects and deadlines scheduled for the coming week. Review your month's pending file on the first day of every month.

CALENDAR

One of the most important tools to help you organize your time is a calendar, a personal schedule of where you need to be and what you need to do. It doesn't matter whether it's a month at a glance, week at a glance, wallet-type Day Timer or electronic calendar. If electronic, be sure its capacity limits you to no less than six entries per day. Many companies now have computerized scheduling calendars. If yours does learn all its capabilities and use it regularly. Carry your calendar or a copy of it with you at all times. Remember to coordinate it with your office calendar, the calendar on your desk, or the one your secretary keeps for you.

FILING SYSTEMS

Department Filing System

In juggling many tasks related to several projects, how do you keep your documents organized? The department filing system is the answer. Ask a secretary to introduce you to it — and walk you through it — for it will give you valuable insight into the way your company or department categorizes and documents projects. Understanding that system allows you access to valuable files. It will also allow you to set up a personal filing system that will mirror your department's filing system.

Now you're ready to set up your personal file. It should imitate the same organization or design of your department's filing system. You'll find what you need more easily that way. The system will enable others to locate necessary documents as well.

Tickle File

A Future Date File, Tickler File or Tickle File, will also prove invaluable to your ability to be organized and not miss deadlines. The tickle file is a file specifically designed to remind you of future activities. This file is not kept by subject, but by date. A well-designed future date file would include thirteen folders: twelve manila folders labeled January through December, and an accordion file with 31 day slots for the current month. On the first day of every month you would empty the contents for "this month" into the dates on which next action will need to be taken: the next call made or next appointment. This file "tickles" your memory for a future date. Many companies have computerized filing systems which include a future date file system. If your department doesn't have a tickle file for you to use, create your own.

LISTS

Lists will keep you on time, prioritized and organized. Keeping two lists will keep you out of trouble: the "To Do" List and the "Boss Communication List."

The "To Do" List

The first is the "To Do" list. Drafted the night before and revised daily, it includes a column to indicate the task and another column to indicate your priorities: A, B, or C or one through five. Throughout the day cross off what you've completed. At the end of the day transfer onto tomorrow's "To Do" list.

File these lists by dropping them into the front of a file folder of old "To Do" lists, providing a permanent record of how you've spent your day. If you have an automated system archive each list. Old "To Do" lists may be valuable in tracing back what day you contacted a business associate, when you completed part of a project, or help you complete an activity report.

PRIORITY 1-3	STATUS	TASK
1		1) prepare memo for John
	done	2) call for status: sales project
2		3) confirm lunch Leo
3	due Wed	4) review mailing chart: call contractor
	4:00 pm	5) check mailing after 4:00
1		6) discuss status; call research; make decision
1	9am Wed	7) call Bob for appt: Wed best
		8) Revise Murphy letter - get mailed
		9) Pick up cleaning
	1:30	10) Marketing Meeting 1:30

Figure 1: The "To Do" list

Boss Communication List

Your second list is a "Boss Communication List." It's an ongoing list, prepared during each day. It's a "talking paper," a list of questions, ideas, or suggestions you think your boss should know about. The purpose of this list is to make you instantly prepared to talk with your boss — without wasting time — in an organized and efficient manner. Your boss may or may not have a lot of time for you. It's not unusual to have a boss who, on the spur of the moment, will invite you to an impromptu meeting or lunch. Have that list ready on a moment-by-moment basis, keeping it going for days on end, if necessary. It may help to have a separate column to note the relevance of any of the subjects you present. You're on a learning curve here. Ask your boss which questions or comments are most important. This will help you know how to focus your energies in the future.

Donna supervised the sorting room of a package delivery company. Her boss, Bruce, told her not to bother him unless it was something she couldn't handle. Donna kept a running list of subjects to discuss with Bruce so she was ready to meet whenever he was. She knew he was like all bosses and wanted to be kept informed of what she was doing, but only wanted the important things. Usually they'd talk daily, but occasionally it would be two or three days before he had time to address her concerns. She dealt with the list in order of importance to Bruce. Time permitting, she'd ask if he wanted to be updated on X, Y or Z topics. She also asked if he wanted to be updated in the future on the things they talked about. After their third update, Bruce said, "Donna, you're the best organized supervisor I have. You get more done using less of my time. I appreciate having you update me on the important issues and giving me time to spend on the problem areas. Keep up the good work; you'll make a good manager."

Discuss with   (NAME OF BOSS)

PRIORITY 1-3	DISCUSS	FUTURE DISCUSS YES/NO
2	Status of mailing chart	Y
1	My decision on product shipping	Y
	Discussion with John	N
3	Problem with printing dept	
	Progress of meetings with marketing	
	Should I call Jones?	
	Day off 15th	

Figure 2: Boss Communication List

CRITICISM: ACCEPTED AND GIVEN

How to Accept It

There will be much more criticism in a business environment than what you experienced in school. Handling criticism is much easier when you accept it as a helpful and necessary ingredient in the mastery of your skills. You'll be working closely with a wide variety of people; criticism will be a vital part of learning about your company, about your job, and how to get along as part of the team. Most people don't give criticism well, nor do they receive it well. With a little practice, these guidelines will help you do both proficiently.

Not "if," but "when" you're criticized, accept it gracefully. It's not easy initially to accept criticism, but it's absolutely necessary to improve. That makes criticism very valuable. Those who accomplish things are going to get criticized. The alternative is to do nothing, to try to make no mistakes. Expect criticism, even welcome it. It means you are doing something, learning and getting more proficient. Develop a way to handle it; to profit from it. Your ability to accept and learn from criticism is an indication of your maturity.

ACCEPT IT

When first criticized step outside the criticism to see it more clearly. The tendency, initially, is to justify and defend. Neither of these two tendencies work. They throw up roadblocks to the person doing the criticizing. The temptation is to see yourself as right; after all, no one sets out to do something wrong. The attitude to develop here is to ask yourself, "If this was someone else I knew, how would I expect them to handle it?" This will put distance between you and the criticism. You performed as you thought best, but now someone is offering you another way. Be open to alternatives.

ADMIT IT

Second, admit right away what has been done. No excuses. No blaming. As soon as you admit it the situation will be instantly diffused and you can begin concentrating on what action you can take to make a correction. "I made a mistake. I'm sorry. What can I do to correct this?" Get the person who has made the criticism "off" the position of criticizing and "into" the positive, a new framework for correcting the situation. Maybe it's simply a correction and not a total change of course. Be able to say, "You're right, that would make it easier (be a cleaner way to approach it, make it more effective)."

THANK THEM
After you've been given the benefit of someone else's experience and their criticism thank them. Acknowledge their help. Most people don't feel very good about having to criticize. If you thank them it will take the sting out of the encounter, changing what could have been an uncomfortable situation for both of you into a positive relationship. They'll feel better about you and about giving you help in the future. We need to encourage those around us to support us and to help us do a better job. Remember this: it is not fun to criticize. Often it's as uncomfortable to criticize another as it is to receive criticism.

DEMONSTRATE CHANGE
Go out of your way to demonstrate you have profited by the criticism or suggestions made to you. When criticism is given, a manager is usually apprehensive and worried that the problem will not be corrected. When the criticism is accepted and significant change is made, both the manager and employee can benefit from the change. That was certainly the case with Donna when she finally spoke candidly with Nikki about her lack of performance.

Donna really cared about her people, encouraged them, coached them and worked hard to set a good example. They liked her and worked hard to please her, all except Nikki. Nikki was pleasant enough, never hostile, but never did more than the minimum required of her. Frustrated, Donna asked Bruce his opinion. She then met with Nikki and explained exactly how Nikki needed to change her performance to keep her job. Donna left the meeting feeling badly for having had to criticize her, and believing Nikki would quit. Not so. Nikki's work significantly improved and she stopped by Donna's desk after nearly every shift to see how she was doing. Within six months, Nikki became one of Donna's best workers.

DEVELOP YOUR OWN METHOD
Take some time to develop your own method of receiving criticism, using some or all of these four steps explained above:

1) Accept it - don't justify or defer
2) Admit it - admit mistakes, ask for help
3) Thank others - create positive relationships
4) Change - demonstrate you have made changes

How To Give Criticism

Now, what happens if it is you who must criticize? How do you go about giving criticism in a positive, creative way? First, be reluctant to criticize until you really know what is going on. It will appear, initially, that there is much to criticize in your company, your department, your co-workers, and your boss. Practice fact-finding by doing a little research before you offer criticism. Ask a third person or a fourth. Get the whole picture first. It may turn out another person was right and you were wrong because you didn't have the whole picture.

HAVE A PLAN
Have a plan and prepare it carefully, rather than offering criticism on the spur of the moment. Be careful of what you say. Practice saying it. Always give criticism in private, never in front of others. Approach it from the standpoint of facts, not from emotions. Criticize the behavior and its results, not the person.

MAKE IT POSITIVE
Sandwich your comments with positive comments. Start and end with positive comments, stating the criticism in between.

ADJUST YOUR CRITICISM
To some people criticism is devastating; to other people it takes a great deal of emphasis before they even realize you're criticizing them. Take into account each person before you speak. Get to know the person and adjust to the individual you are criticizing so you aren't "blowing someone away" or "offering an irrelevancy."

Cory prepared a memo for his boss's signature which contained several errors. Cory's new secretary had distributed the memo to several senior managers with neither the approval nor signature of his boss. Cory knew his secretary to be conscientious, but realized her inexperience and planned how to tell her that she had made an error. He knew she was sensitive, soft-spoken and so he planned in advance what to say. He practiced at his desk before calling her into his office. "Everyone did a good job of getting the memo out last night. Thanks for staying. There was a problem, though, in that the memo was never corrected or signed by my boss. There were some errors and now I'm in hot water. I'd like to go over what happened and come up with a procedure so we don't send out another memo without final approval and signature. You're doing a good job for me; I appreciate your dedication to your job."

Cory spent less than ten minutes preparing, but the criticism was well-received and strengthened their relationship. The next memo was carefully laid on his desk for proofing and signature.

COMPLIMENTS AND ACKNOWLEDGEMENTS

Giving Compliments

The ability to give sincere compliments and praise is extremely important to your success in business. Paying compliments and giving praise have the effect of endearing us to others. We're all motivated by praise. The higher up we find ourselves on the management ladder, the more important will be our need to learn how to sincerely compliment others. This is one of our most important management tools. Cultivate this skill by practicing the first day on the job — and every day thereafter. Allow this skill to become a part of who you are. This will also help in developing your most important skill, creating positive relationships.

How do you develop this skill? Practice first in your personal life. Become more aware of the positive. Only compliment when you appreciate something. Be sincere. Be specific. "Nice job," sounds good, but it doesn't reveal what you really noticed and doesn't sound sincere. Better to say: *"You were well prepared on that presentation, George; I learned a lot about our product distribution." Always attempt to use the name of the person you are complimenting.*

It's safer if you steer clear of personal appearances: how people look or how they dress. Confine your compliments and praise to areas of business and job accomplishments. The best attitude in developing the unique skill of paying sincere compliments is to recognize that everyone does something good each day. Your job is to look for it, recognize it and compliment it.

Acknowledging Others

Acknowledgement is any brief greeting. It recognizes that others exist by either a smile, a nod, or in calling them by name and speaking with them. Acknowledging others is very important to your business image. Many employees will form their opinions of you by whether you say hello or smile. If you acknowledge others, those who don't know you will think you're friendly, a nice person, happy and in a good mood. If you don't acknowledge others, people who don't know you will think you're unfriendly, disinterested, a loner and moody.

To be sure you are perceived as friendly, you should acknowledge everyone every time you see them. It may only be with a comment and a smile: keep your eyes up, don't look at the floor. Additionally, make a point to say, "Good morning," to everyone the first time you see them every day. Be especially conscious of people with lower job status. Everyone remembers to greet the boss. Learn people's names and use them in your acknowledgements. Stop and chat sometimes with people, be friendly, find out what they're interested in.

You can test the importance of acknowledgements by watching the senior managers that have reputations of being nice people. They will make a habit of acknowledging people. Compare them to the top managers who maintain reputations of being difficult to work for; they will usually ignore acknowledgements.

What Grads Should Know:

NEW SKILLS
*These skills are important business talents that take significant time and effort to develop. Start now and continue throughout your career to refine these skills.

ORGANIZATION
*Priorities, deadlines and workloads are so significant in business that you must use these aids for your benefit:
-1) the personal schedule calendar
-2) filing systems
-3) future date file
-4) personal lists including the "To Do" list, the "Boss Communication" list

CRITICISM: ACCEPTED AND GIVEN
*Learn to positively receive criticism using the four steps:
-1) accepting
-2) admitting
-3) thanking
-4) demonstrating change

*Learn to give positive criticism by:
-1) planning
-2) privatizing
-3) sandwiching the negative between positives
-4) adjusting it to the individual.

COMPLIMENTS AND ACKNOWLEDGEMENTS
*Learn and practice the art of sincere praise. This
skill is often overlooked by grads but will be
instrumental in your success.
*Acknowledging everyone every time you see them
will create an important, positive impression with
employees you don't know.

Chapter 5

DESIRABLE TRAITS

There are several basic personality traits important to all employees of all businesses. If you already have these traits you are fortunate; if you don't they may be developed. This chapter describes each trait and explains how it is desirable in business.

POSITIVE ATTITUDE

Common to every company is the shared ideal of maintaining a positive attitude. Since this "positive, can-do" attitude is so highly prized, it's worth observing, understanding and developing.

All things being equal, if there is a promotion to be given it will often be given to the employee with the positive attitude over the employee lacking it. So what is it, how do you acquire it and how do you develop it? The key word to understanding and developing a positive attitude is "willingness." It is the willingness and enthusiasm to do the work given you, to finish it and to ask for more. It's the ability to keep in mind the company's goals and to do whatever is necessary to get things done while maintaining a friendly and helpful demeanor. People with positive attitudes don't waste time complaining about what's wrong. They concentrate on what's necessary to become successful. They neither criticize nor do they find fault. They recognize a problem, see it as a challenge and look for solutions to resolve it.

This is a trait you need to observe and acquire immediately. It is also a trait you'll want to develop continually throughout your career. The added benefit to you is that there is not an aspect of life where this positive attitude will not prove valuable. Whether in your personal life as a friend, sibling or spouse, or as you advance in your business career, this attitude will help you to achieve or to exceed your goals.

Identify a Positive Attitude

Become aware of your co-workers, your friends and yourself. First, be observant of others' comments. Are they critical and fault-finding or are they problem-solving and forward-looking? Analyze your own comments and determine if they are positive, problem-solving and goal-oriented. It is possible to express a dilemma in a positive way. If you are prone to complaining or criticizing this is a crucial behavior to change. Those who don't have a positive attitude normally are not responsive to change. They only understand that their future somehow looks dismal and things aren't going their way. They have missed out on the hopeful, helpful willingness that creates an attitude for problem-solving. Monitor yourself daily and observe your own positive attitude. That was one of the things Jake noticed about the new production manager, Pam. She had quickly gained a positive reputation within the company because of her solution to a third-shift production problem.

Pam had observed that, of the plant's three shifts, the midnight shift continued to under-perform. She'd observed the grumbling about the mistakes and general discontent the workers felt. Company goals had been recently communicated to each of the three shifts in hopes it would increase production. Still, workers on the midnight shift remained unmotivated and produced inferior work. Absenteeism was high and other workers were continually asked to cover for missing workers.

Pam decided to spend several nights working third shift to observe the managers and employees to see if she could identify what was wrong. She walked around the plant and talked to the superintendent, all supervisors and many of the older employees. After two shifts it became apparent that the night superintendent was the problem. He was a suspicious, negative person who lacked confidence and distrusted his supervisors and employees. He tried to control by fear and intimidation.

Pam moved him to the first shift as a special projects manager and promoted the best supervisor to night superintendent. The improvement was amazing; within a month the third shift had equalled the production of the second shift. Jake was impressed with Pam's decisive solution and positive results. Now here was a manager he could learn from!

Positive people with problem-solving attitudes are typically forward-moving. They're the ones who will be promoted. Because they're not negative themselves they spend their energy staying focused on the positive and constructive. In this way they accumulate more successes and develop added confidence in their own abilities to do their jobs.

Develop a Positive Attitude

Although some people may be born with a positive attitude most of us have to develop it. The best way to create and maintain a positive attitude is to first be aware of who is positive and who is negative — including your own tendencies. How do positive people make suggestions? How do you make suggestions? How do positive people report a problem? How do you report a problem?

It is possible to change a negative suggestion into a positive one by starting your comments with a solution. The idea is to learn how to turn a potentially negative response into a positive by stating the solution first. Learn from Jake how to restructure a negative response.

Jake burst into Pam's office, knowing he had to tell her first. "We've got a problem with those paint sets. The address labels going to the West Coast are all wrong. I know they're supposed to be in today's mail, but there's no way. The computer services department can reprint the labels; maybe we can get them out tomorrow."

Later that day Pam called Jake in. "You gave me quite a scare today, Jake. I thought we'd lost the whole $20,000 order this morning when you said, "We've got a problem with the paint sets." I know you've got your hands full, and you are an asset to this department in your efforts to coordinate with other departments. But I'm going to ask you to consider telling me your solutions up front when you're reporting problems to me. You're one of my best, Jake, and every time I see you I want to think of you as a problem-solver, not the bearer of bad news. It's a subtle but extremely important trait, a skill I've had to develop and I know it's one you can develop also. It will give me more confidence in you. Start out by telling me your positive solution to correct the problem. Instead of hitting me with the problem and making me sweat, just tell me how you've planned to remedy it. I'll expect the positive from you that way. You'll be doing yourself a favor. I won't say, 'Oh no, here comes a problem.' I'll say, 'He's got it handled.' "

Jake heard Pam. On the drive home that night he reflected on what she'd told him about sharing the solution to the problem with her immediately and helping her avoid additional stress. He could have easily rephrased it. He'd wanted her to know he was concerned. That's why he'd told her as he did; he wanted her to know the problem was a large one and that he'd taken the initiative to fix it. He would catch himself in future difficulties and rephrase, offering the solution to the problem first: "Pam, I've asked computer services to reprint our West Coast mailing labels so we can get out today's mailing. They were printed incorrectly. The mailing will only be one day off target." It wasn't that hard to rephrase it positively.

Create a Positive Image

The image others have of you is based on your attitude about your work and is communicated through your actions in nearly everything you say and do during your day. Become aware of the overall image others have of you. Ask yourself, "How can I present this situation in a positive way? How would I like to have it presented to me with the least amount of stress and grief?" Your efforts in turning each statement into a positive one, together with your positive attitude toward your work will create an overall positive image. That very image will help you be noticed and appreciated.

GENERAL KNOWLEDGE

Being a business person, you'll now be expected to know about 1) current events and sports, 2) business in general, 3) and especially your industry and your company. There is no time like the present to develop a lifelong interest in these topics. Keeping alert and aware of current events will prepare you to participate in social situations and business lunches which require your opinion and comments.

Current Events

Recommended reading for national and international current events includes, minimally, *The Wall Street Journal,* one half-hour news program daily, such as *CNN News*, and one weekly news magazine, such as *Time* or *Newsweek*.

Sports

If local sports teams are popular with your employees or customers, general knowledge of sports can be very helpful in talking with business people when you don't know their backgrounds or interests. Read one newspaper sports page and one sports magazine weekly, such as *Sports Illustrated*.

Local Events

Don't forget to read about local news, local sports and events, minimally the front page of business and sports sections. Those who don't keep current look as though they don't know what is happening. Throughout the local paper you may even find references to friends and families of those with whom you'll be associated with in business.

Business

For business news read *The Wall Street Journal* and one weekly or monthly business magazine, such as *Business Week* or *Fortune Magazine*.

Trade magazines are also very helpful. There are certain things you should know, and many items you'll need in order to keep current. Get on your company's or department's routing list of publications addressing your industry. Take them home and read them. Become aware of competing companies, problems and current trends inherent in your industry.

Business jargon, which is the terminology particular to your industry, is important to understand as quickly as possible. There will be abbreviations and words you'll not be familiar with initially. Ask lots of questions; it's easier in the beginning because no one will expect you to know the jargon.

While you are reading be alert for articles of specific interest to people at work. Recognize how important it is for others to be recognized or to have their family's achievements recognized.

Donna realized this on Monday morning as she arrived her usual five minutes early for the weekly staff meeting. Bruce, smiling, was talking with Al, whose orders she knew had been delayed last week. She'd expected tension, at the least, and the potential of a major confrontation. "Thanks for the clipping," she overheard Bruce say as he held up a copy of the newspaper story Al had just given him, waving it at her. "Did you see my son's picture in the Sunday paper? He scored 22 points in Saturday's game." Donna said, "No, I missed it. Congratulations. Let me read it. You must be very proud of him." Darn, she thought, I'm going to have to start reading the sports page, especially during basketball season.

CONTROL OF ANGER

In nearly all cases the best action to take when you are ready to explode in anger is to suppress it. Temper and anger are luxuries you simply can't afford in business.

When the steam begins to build from anger, remember to keep your mouth shut until you cool down. Count to ten — or one hundred — if necessary. Exercise. Run up or down several flights of stairs. Write down what's eating at you. Remember, you are developing positive relationships, not enemies.

Diffusing Anger

When a supervisor or boss demonstrates anger, back off and let them cool down. There are two situations in which you might find yourself caught in an angry backfire: someone is angry with you, or they are angry and blowing off steam around you for a reason unrelated to you. Anger emerges when someone is feeling frustrated, when they're wrong or when they've made a mistake. Often their anger will have nothing to do with you or your relationship and will emerge in the midst of talking about something totally unrelated. Sometimes they'll return and apologize to you later. Bruce, a seasoned yet emotional middle manager I once knew, is the best example.

One day Bruce stomped by Donna's desk, "I want to see you in my office, now!" That's unlike him, *she thought as she pulled the door closed behind her, her heart pounding. His voice boomed, "What happened to those special order crates sitting on the loading dock? They should have gone out this morning!" Donna replied, "I didn't know they were still here, I'll check it out." Bruce shot back, "Why don't you know what's going on in your department? Do you expect me to do your job and mine?"*

Donna realized her defensiveness was causing Bruce to get madder. She looked at the floor for a few seconds, and after catching her breath and regaining her composure, she tried a new tact: "You're right, Bruce, I blew it, I let you down. I'm sorry. I'll get them out on the next truck."

She was able to get them out and meant to tell Bruce, but he caught her as he was rushing out. "I'm sorry I blew up, Donna. It's been a really bad day. I know you're doing a good job, but when I saw those special orders I lost it. I should know not to take out unrelated personal problems on my best people. Thanks for listening to my outburst and taking care of the problem." It was then that Donna realized it wasn't her performance, nor even the delay in shipping which had caused Bruce's outburst. She now realized the tension he was experiencing was unrelated to her work. Donna decided to try to be more aware of Bruce's moods and to be careful what she said when he was having problems.

CONFORMING

Fitting In

There are significantly more adjustments you'll have to make in business than in school. In school you were encouraged to express yourself, to be unique and explore your potential. In business you are being paid to fit in, to conform. Every company has its image. By accepting the job you are buying into that image. You're competing with others who have already proven they can fit in. Conformity signals to management that you understand what is expected and you acknowledge and accept their standards. Your daily behavior and overall image must fit into the company image that already exists, especially that presented by higher management. You can judge yourself to have been successful if senior management thinks you conform to their standards.

Being Different

Management will be uncomfortable with whoever stands out as   different from their image, different from the norm. It's often these employees who will not follow the rules. If you step outside of that image it will raise questions in their minds about whether or not you will be able to make the essential adjustments and changes. There's a flexibility required on the part of employees — an ability to adjust — to appear as part of the team. Remember, your promotions will be based on senior management's perception of whether or not you have senior management potential.

PATIENCE

Patience will be required throughout your career, but many grads find the first year or two especially trying. The change from school's constant measurements with tests, grades and changing classes to the more long-term, stable business environment is hard for some grads to adjust to. In business you may be formally evaluated once a year instead of twice a quarter as you were in school.

Expect this change to try your patience. Just relax and concentrate on all the new things you have to learn about your job, company and developing positive relationships.

HUMOR

Humor is much more important in business than it was in school. Humor relieves stress and can contribute to others' enjoyment of their jobs.

There are a number of reasons why humor will prove beneficial to you. It makes you more attractive to others, helps you enjoy your work more, motivates others in their work, breaks tension in difficult situations and converts problem people into team players.

Be especially careful of how, when and around whom you use humor. Listen and learn what is acceptable and appropriate. Wait until you are comfortable with people before you use it. Be aware of the extreme jokester who can become the office clown.

CHANGE

Change is inherent in business. Business is in a state of constant change, moving toward the goals of becoming more efficient, more effective and lowering costs. With the inundation of technological improvements and inventions the pace of change has escalated. What's interesting is that while business naturally changes to grow better, human nature adamantly opposes change. As humans we prefer familiar, established procedures, especially older employees who are more comfortable with the status quo.

Management looks for employees, therefore, who are not only capable of innovation but who are the least reluctant to change. Who wants to distribute work to someone who will be resistant? An excellent way to please managers is to eagerly accept new projects, procedures or equipment and to thrive on change. Develop the reputation that you look forward to the new, the different.

What Grads Should Know

POSITIVE ATTITUDE
   *All companies want grads with a positive attitude, which is a willingness and enthusiasm to complete all work given and to ask for more. Be friendly and helpful; concentrate on solving problems and accomplishing goals.

   *Develop A Positive Attitude
      Be aware of the impression you make on others. Make comments positive; begin reports to your

manager with a solution. Avoid complaints and criticism.

*Create A Positive Image
Others will want to work with you and management will want to give you the most important work; this will help you achieve promotions faster.

GENERAL KNOWLEDGE
*As a business person you must stay current of business in general, including your company and industry, and current events and sports.

CONTROL OF ANGER
*Anger is a luxury grads can't afford in business. Learn to control it.

CONFORMING
*Management will judge you by how well you adjust to the image and values of the company. They have the money, it's your job to conform.

PATIENCE
*Grads need patience to change from college's constant feedback to business' limited feedback (annual performance evaluations).

HUMOR
*Using or developing your sense of humor helps you enjoy business and encourages others to like you. It can also help you influence and motivate others.

CHANGE

*Competition in business requires constant change. Push yourself to eagerly accept change. Management will reward those who welcome change.

Chapter 6

YOUR BOSS

Quick Reference

- Choice of Term "Boss"
- Importance of Your Boss
- Interdependence: Boss and Graduate
- What Your Boss Expects from You
- Your Boss is Human
- Your Boss as Mentor
- Disagreements with Your Boss
- What Grads Should Know

Your boss is the single-most important person in your relationship with your company. It is this critical relationship that will get you promoted or not. After reading this chapter you'll know what your boss expects and what you can expect of her. You'll learn what you can do in your work to win her over and move toward that first promotion.

CHOICE OF TERM "BOSS"

Most modern management and business text books have stopped using the old-fashioned word "boss." They say it's too authoritarian and not in tune with modern participatory management. It is supposed to indicate absolute-rule decisions rather than the modern "agreement among team members." Some companies have replaced the word "boss" with "lead associate" and "employee" with "associate" to reflect their equal status.

I choose to use the more harsh word "boss" rather than the more common terms — manager or supervisor — in this chapter particularly to emphasize to the graduate the importance in business of your boss. This is done intentionally to counteract a common mistake made by grads: that is, not realizing the extent of authority and importance of their bosses to them and to their careers.

IMPORTANCE OF YOUR BOSS

There is only one person in the company who has enough information to judge you. Others hear part or see part, but they don't know your work well enough to judge how you've handled what's been assigned. Graduates who are successful understand what a powerful position their boss holds and adjust as necessary to accommodate the importance of this position. Regardless of whether you get along with your boss, like your boss, or respect your boss, your boss is the "single most important person" in your organization as far as your career is concerned.

To make a comparison to school, your boss is as important to you now as all of your professors in college and your grades rolled into one. Without them you wouldn't have graduated. Without your boss you won't get promoted.

If this weren't important enough, additionally it is your boss who is your vital communications link with others within the various departments of your company. And if that weren't enough, it is also she who sets your workload, goals and standards. As you can see, your boss is very important to you.

Your contact with other department heads and senior management will necessarily be limited. You'll see them on the elevator or when they walk past your desk. They don't know about you, but they trust your boss. She has credibility with them. It is your boss who advises others in management as to what you've done. It is your boss who knows the rules and what's going on in the rest of the company. It is your boss upon whom you will rely as your source of information, as will others rely on her as their source of information about you.

In school you had perhaps forty or fifty classes and over thirty different professors. All of those people assigned your work, made decisions on your performance and gave you grades. When all are combined, they can be compared to how important your boss currently is to you. You may well have the same boss for four years (as compared to four years of school), maybe even longer. Your career will be judged by that person. There is no one else as influential to you and your career as your boss.

INTERDEPENDENCE
BETWEEN
BOSS AND GRADUATE

Many graduates don't realize how important they are to their boss. Your boss is under the same expectations to perform as you are. Your boss depends on the important duties that you must do well so she can be promoted. Your boss is responsible to make sure your work gets done as well and as fast as possible. Your success or failure is ultimately her success or failure.

Also, your boss's most important management abilities will be judged by how well you do. Your actions are a direct reflection on your boss's abilities to:

1) Evaluate and select employees
2) Teach and develop employees
3) Manage and motivate employees
4) Provide positive leadership and a role model for employees

If you are successful your boss will be considered good at these key managerial skills. If you don't succeed your boss's management skills will be questioned. Your boss is dependent upon your performance and highly motivated to make sure you are successful in your new job.

WHAT YOUR BOSS EXPECTS FROM YOU

Habits, Skills and Traits

As a starting point, your boss expects your best efforts in the subjects we have discussed in the chapters on good work habits, new skills and desirable traits. The specific levels of excellence described in these chapters may actually be expected by few bosses and wholly achieved by few graduates, but the list provides a good basis for the subjects on which each grad will be evaluated. Use the subjects as your guide for what your boss will prefer, if not expect.

No Surprises, or Communicate!

One of the most important expectations of every boss is to be kept informed of what their employees are doing. This is especially important for graduates because they have not yet worked out what is and what is not important to their bosses. One of the first discussions your new boss has with you will probably include the words "no surprises." This means keep your boss informed of what you're doing. If you get into trouble or cause any problems, she can help to fix it or help you to remedy the situation, but only if she knows what's going on. Better yet, communicate enough of what you intend to do so your boss can advise you before problems arise. There are several variables that determine what needs to be communicated and how much time to spend in communicating.

WHAT TO COMMUNICATE
It is difficult to generalize about what to inform your boss about and what is a waste of her time. The following guidelines will be instructive.

1) What your boss wants or needs to know: some like a great deal of detail about everything you're doing; others will only want to hear if you're in trouble. As a general rule, when you start out lean towards over-communicating with your boss until you sort out the level of information your boss wants.

2) The type of work you're doing: is your work all within your department, or does it give you exposure to other departments, employees, customers, etc? As a general rule, communicate more when you work outside your department.

3) Your diplomacy: do you have good diplomatic skills or do you tend to offend people? Be sensitive to this and be aware of your diplomacy skills. As a general rule, grads with poor diplomacy skills should communicate more.

4) Company atmosphere: is this a large, very political company or a small, informal company with few political considerations? As a general rule, the more politically sensitive your company is, the more you should communicate.

HOW TO COMMUNICATE

1) Tell your boss you realize communication is important and would like her help. Additionally, ask her for general guidelines on what she does and doesn't expect to be told.

2) Be organized. Use your "Boss Communication" list explained in New Skills, chapter 4, to consistently be ready to discuss the status of what you are doing. Make notes on your list whether or not your boss wants to hear about a particular subject; file these comments for future reference.

It will probably take time for you and your new boss to work out the amount and type of communication she prefers. That's what Fred realized in working with Ellie, his first boss.

Fred had been concentrating at his desk all morning when Ellie stopped by. "Fred, I have a staff meeting in fifteen minutes. Please come in and give me an update on your bond project; it may come up in the meeting and I need to know what's happening." Fred grabbed his communication list and followed

Ellie into her office. He briefed her on the status of the project. After a minute or two Ellie asked, "What's the participation rate you're requesting?" Fred answered hesitantly, "Seventy percent, same as last year." Ellie pushed back in her chair, "I know that was last year's rate, but that's too high for this year; I'll have to get you the new rate." Fred was glad for the opening, "That's one of the things on my list to discuss with you."

Ellie knew Fred to be conscientious, "I know we haven't had enough time to discuss what you're doing; let's meet every afternoon at 5:00 to review what's going on, OK?" With that she stood up and Fred knew the rest of his list could wait until the next evening. They hadn't been spending enough time communicating and it was a load off his mind to know that she understood. Now they'd have a regularly scheduled time to discuss his projects and time to sort out what should and shouldn't be communicated.

Loyalty

An equally important expectation of every boss is loyalty.

Most would define loyalty as a higher degree of care, concern and commitment to your boss than to any other person in your business. (The only concerns higher than this would be those for family and personal relationships or personal principles such as moral and ethical standards.) In other words, if it doesn't conflict with your personal relationships and ethical standards, then your boss's interests and well-being come before all other people in your company and industry. That would include high-level management, suppliers and customers as well as the public.

Fred, fortunately, was aware of this when he accidently overheard two managers talking as he walked to the parking lot after work. One he recognized as the vice president of finance. "We're going to cut the training staff by 50% to lower costs," is what he thought he heard.

Now, Fred knew that the entire training staff reported to his boss, Ellie. He agonized throughout the evening if he should say anything, and if so, exactly what he should or shouldn't say. It had been a private conversation he'd overheard; had he heard it correctly? Would he put his career in jeopardy for repeating what he thought he'd heard?

After a restless night he decided over morning coffee to tell Ellie. After all, she was his boss. This bit of news would make a significant difference in the planning and budgeting she was currently involved in. It was important that he be loyal to her. He would have to trust her not to get him involved for eavesdropping. He also decided to protect himself just a bit by re-phrasing his information in the form of a question.

In the hallway he asked Ellie if he might speak with her privately and she drew the door closed behind them once inside the office. "Should I tell you about what I accidently heard the V.P. of finance say about cuts in training?" Fred asked. He knew that would give her a way out if the information leak would pose problems. It turned out that Ellie was aware of the pending cuts based on budget projections. Fred was relieved. The way he'd presented the information and the loyalty he showed Ellie raised him several notches in her perception, however. Ellie pegged Fred as someone who had her best interests in mind and who would be loyal to her if she needed it.

Loyalty to your boss is very important. You should take every opportunity to demonstrate ways you consider your boss's best interests can be served. Also be aware of your own best interests and those of your company and customers. If you have conflicting loyalties or ethics, ask a parent or friend who has had business experience but who is not directly related to your company or situation. Their perceptions and suggestions can often prove valuable in warding off potential mistakes.

YOUR BOSS IS HUMAN

Some grads make the assumption that their boss always has the good of the company in mind, that they have the highest standards (above personal interests). Bosses are people and people are human. Your boss is going to have all the normal feelings of any other human being. Treat your boss first as a human being and second as a business person. Try to look at everything from the human nature viewpoint first, business second. If you forget the human and personal side you will error as did Fred the day Ellie's son drove to pick her up for lunch.

It was about 12:20 when John arrived; Fred greeted him and said, "I think your Mom has already gone to lunch." John's smile faded, "Gosh, I thought I was going to have lunch with her today." Fred felt awkward, he knew Ellie had a manager's staff lunch today so he told John, "I think she's gone; it's already twenty after. Do you want to come back after lunch?" John left and agreed to call later in the afternoon.

A few minutes later Ellie returned, obviously rushed. "Have you seen my son? I told him I'd have lunch with him today." Fred admitted seeing him, "I'm sorry, I told him I thought you'd already gone. I just assumed you were at the manager's lunch." Now Ellie was noticeably disturbed. Her son was important to her and she'd been working hard to spend more time with him lately. "No, I decided to make an excuse and skip the lunch."

Luckily, John called back within a few minutes and they were able to meet at a nearby restaurant. No damage done. Fred thought about how he could have handled it differently.

He thought of the importance of the mother-son relationship. He could have sat John down and told him he'd look for his mom. He could have gone up to the staff meeting and given her a note that her son was there. The moral to the story: always first consider your boss as a human being. When you do this, family is usually more important than business.

Step outside the immediate business situation and look at your boss from the human point of view. How would you want someone to cover for you?

YOUR BOSS AS MENTOR

Boss's Decision

Part of your boss's job is to know your career goals and advise you of opportunities that may be available within the company. Many grads confuse these two basic career development duties with being a mentor. A mentor will go beyond asking about your job interests; a mentor will take an active interest in helping your advancement by advising you how to get ahead and promoting your capabilities to management.

Your boss may or may not choose to be your mentor; it's her decision. Choosing to be a mentor is always a one-sided decision. The mentor makes the decision.

There is a popular misconception among grads that they choose someone to be a mentor and career advancement automatically becomes easier. In reality, to be of any value a mentor must be personally motivated to help the grad and to take the time and make the effort to be of help. If your boss — or any other manager — is to be of value as a mentor it must be her decision.

Mentor's Self-Interest

To encourage a boss or other manager to become your mentor it is necessary to demonstrate your ability to make her look good. A mentor will choose the best employee that will help the company and at the same time make her look good in doing so. Managers are judged on their ability to select the best employees. Most managers will be eager to act as mentor to the best employees so they will get the reputation of being a good judge of talent.

The other part of self-interest is personal rapport. Managers will choose grads they personally like and feel comfortable with. If your boss likes you and thinks you are the best employee, you have a good opportunity to acquire her as a mentor.

DISAGREEMENT WITH YOUR BOSS

As a general rule, the best solution for any disagreement with your boss is for you to make whatever adjustment is required to resolve the problem. This is the best solution because it's usually in your best interests over the long term. During the first few years in business the grad usually doesn't have the experience and frame of reference to judge whether the boss or grad's actions are outside of acceptable norms. If the disagreement is so significant that the grad feels incapable of adjusting there are three steps which should be followed to try to resolve the disagreement:

1) Seek experienced outside advice
2) Discuss privately with your boss, after step one
3) Ask your boss for the name of someone with
   whom you can discuss the problem.

First, seek experienced outside advice. If you are not able to adjust to what your boss wants, seek advice from a person you know who is not connected to your company in any way. Be sure they have at least five years of experience in business. Try to be honest and impartial when explaining the problem. Try to take this person's advice. This process of talking it out will be an opportunity to gain insight into your boss's personality and preferences.

Second, if you are unable to take the advice of an outside person, or if the issue remains unresolved, select the right time and place for a private discussion of the subject with your boss. Be objective and ask for her help in resolving the dilemma. Try out your boss's solution.

Third, if you can not adjust to your boss's resolution, ask your boss for the name of someone within your company with whom you can discuss the issue. Meet with that person, discuss it honestly, take his advice.

Fred tapped on Ellie's office door lightly, he knew she'd been in meetings all day and had returned just five minutes before their 5:00 meeting. After a quick update and one question, Ellie changed the subject and told him about how their company was forming a development team for a new product in their west coast office. "It would be a good opportunity for you, Fred. Just four months, a change of pace, you'd learn a lot. . . ." Fred had reasons for not wanting to leave, but they were more personal than business-related. "I'm just concerned about being gone so long," he managed. "To be honest, your work is easier to give to others and you're the only one I can spare from this department," Ellie responded. They left it with no commitment when Fred excused himself, "Can I think about this tonight, Ellie?"

Fred decided not to confront Ellie. After all, she was a good boss; he liked her and she'd always been fair to him. He decided to get some outside advice. He called his next door neighbor, Jack, who was a good friend and had a lot of business experience. Jack said he could refuse to go, but he might lose his job or, at the very least, delay any upcoming promotion. "I'd go and try to make the best of it."

Fred tossed and turned all night, awaking more tired than if he'd not slept at all. Maybe Ellie could find someone else in their department to go to the west coast. That afternoon he suggested just that. Ellie didn't change her mind and was becoming impatient with Fred's unwillingness to go. Ellie referred him to their H.R. Manager. "Take the assignment. Do the best job you can," he advised. ". . . it'll be the best experience you can get for your next step up, and we need you."

Fred finally decided he had no choice; he took the temporary assignment on the west coast. The project turned out to be a success and, contrary to looking forward to returning to the midwest, he loved the ocean and asked to stay on with the new product. After six months it was clear he had the most experience and was promoted. He and Ellie had chances to meet or talk occasionally. Both laughed at how he'd almost missed his big opportunity by digging in his heels. He was glad he'd talked it over with a couple of well-chosen business people, weighing the variables.

What Grads Should Know:

IMPORTANCE OF YOUR BOSS
*This single-most important person in your new
company controls your success.

INTERDEPENDENCE BETWEEN BOSS AND GRAD
*Your boss's success depends on you and the results
of your best efforts. Your boss wants you to
succeed.

WHAT YOUR BOSS EXPECTS FROM YOU
*Good work habits, newly developed skills and
      desirable traits
*Communication (no surprises)
*Personal loyalty (commitment to your boss).

YOUR BOSS IS HUMAN
*Always consider your boss from the viewpoint of a
      human being.

DISAGREEMENT WITH YOUR BOSS
*Use a Three-Step Process to resolve disagreements
      with your Boss
      -Seek outside advise
      -Discuss privately with your boss
      -Ask boss for referral for discussion

Chapter 7

YOUR BOSS'S MANAGING STYLE

QUICK REFERENCE

- Identify Your Boss's Style
- Description of Management Stereotypes:
    Authoritarian
    Consensus
- Your Boss's Preference
- Managing Style Indicators
- Understanding Your Boss's Style
- What is Your Managing Style?
- What Grads Should Know

Understanding your boss's managing style is an important step in establishing a positive relationship. This chapter explains the two management style stereotypes, thereby giving you a comparison to help identify your boss's style. Being able to identify your boss's style and adjusting to it will make you more successful in your first job.

IDENTIFY YOUR BOSS'S STYLE

A good place to start understanding your boss is to identify his managing style so that you can adapt to his way of managing. If you recognize the two common management style stereotypes you can begin to compare your boss's own unique style. The two types are: 1) authoritarian (decision is made by boss's individual judgement), and 2) consensus (decision is made by group agreement).

Your boss probably won't exactly fit either one of these stereotypes, but will include some of each along with other individual traits. Until you become more experienced at identifying managing traits, start with comparing your boss to these two basic types.

DESCRIPTION OF
MANAGEMENT STEREOTYPES

Authoritarian Stereotype

The Authoritarian manager believes:

COMPETITION
Competition makes us strive to be the best. It's exciting and makes us all better. To survive in business you must continue to be better than your competition. If you win you feel great; if you lose you try harder the next time. In competition aggressive people are rewarded. To be the best we must constantly strive to be better than others.

LEADERSHIP

Clear, concise decisions are made by one manager. If someone disagrees he is told the success of the entire team requires he conform and do his best. The manager works the hardest, sets the example and leads the team, showing the team members that the manager cares about every member. The manager is loyal to the team and earns team loyalty. Winning as a team justifies individual sacrifices.

TEAMWORK

If everyone does his job well, speed, efficiency and execution will create a successful outcome. Everyone gives 100% at work. Personal opinions and objections are to be saved for after work. Team members express their opinions before a decision is made; after a decision everyone supports the decision and does his best to achieve the objective. Conforming to team rules and image helps the team function together and be successful.

ORGANIZATION

The most efficient and effective organization is one where final decisions are made by one person, even if that person doesn't always make the very best decision. The speed, efficiency and execution of the decision can make an "OK" decision the best decision. Single person authority can change decisions faster if errors are made. (If we take the time to gain consensus from every team member we'll never get anything done.)

DECISION MAKING

Boss and staff meet to discuss alternatives and consequences. Every person gets a chance to voice his opinion and make recommendations. The boss makes the decision based on his own judgement. All or some of the staff may agree or disagree.

However, the boss is responsible for the decision and its consequences.

Consensus Stereotype

The Consensus manager believes:

COMPETITION
Excessive competition makes enemies and damages relationships. To be the best we must create a cooperative, harmonious atmosphere where everyone is encouraged to do his best. If everyone treats each other fairly we will accomplish more together as a team. Competition creates suspicion, distrust and self-interest rather than achieving team goals. All team members and the team itself wins when we share and compromise.

LEADERSHIP
The manager is a facilitator to help team members reach an agreement (or consensus). A good leader treats all team members fairly and equally. The team is like a family, creating harmonious relationships through personal caring and friendships. Each member's opinion is important and decisions are based on consensus. Team members are loyal to the manager because they are all "friends." Positive relationships enable the team to be successful.

TEAMWORK
Because all team members agree on decisions, the entire team will work toward the goal and be successful. All members should treat each other fairly and equally, creating a positive atmosphere. Soliciting opinions of all team players will ensure the team makes the best decision. The team takes the time to make sure everyone understands and agrees with team goals.

Individual opinions are important and to be a good team member you need to express yourself.

ORGANIZATION
The best organization is one where everyone agrees on a decision. Consensus — based on the entire team — will produce the best decision and the highest level of member commitment to team goals. Treating all team members fairly and equally creates a friendly atmosphere where everyone will do a better job. One-person decisions not only create ill will within the team, but these decisions are not likely to be the best decisions.

DECISION MAKING
The boss and employees meet to discuss decisions. Employees discuss alternatives while the manager gives opinions and acts as group leader, or facilitator, in order to build consensus of agreement for a final decision. All team members are treated fairly and convinced of a "best" decision. Boss determines when this consensus exists on the best decision, with as many team members as possible in agreement.

YOUR BOSS'S PREFERENCE

To understand your boss's decision-making process, listen to what your boss says and what other employees say during a decision-making meeting. Be especially aware of how experienced employees disagree with your boss. The nature and extent of disagreement permitted by your boss is a good indicator of your boss's style. Also, how long a discussion is permitted will be another indicator of the process. A short meeting with little discussion is indicative of the authoritarian process. A long meeting with extensive discussion is indicative of the consensus approach. Those two observations on Paulette's part provided her with the clues she needed to understand how her boss made decisions. To be successful in this company she would need to fit into this model.

The meeting started with Charlie, Paulette's manager, asking for a summary of each sales rep's monthly sales volume. As each reported, Charlie asked for their individual opinions and their customers' reactions to the newly introduced Alaska parka. Hearing concern from several reps over the high price, Charlie explained his belief in future high-end ski clothing. "The decision about this line has been made and I want each of you to concentrate on selling this particular parka. If we work together as a team we'll make it a success, and it will make us a lot of money." A few reps voiced their opinion that selling more of the lower cost parkas could be more profitable. But Charlie, glancing at his watch, ended the meeting by saying, "This is my decision and in the long run this high-end market will be best for this region and best for all of us."

Later that afternoon, after the other sales reps had left, Charlie called Paulette into his office to talk. "Paulette, since you're a trainee, you've not yet acquired a territory. I wanted to take this opportunity to explain what was going on in the meeting this morning. My Washington state sales group is like a sports team. When I make a call like this the whole team pitches in and as long as all of us do our individual best job we'll win. There are several different plays that we can win with — the key is that everyone has to work together with whatever decision is made — and not waste time disagreeing. That's one of the main reasons this region has been a leader in outdoor clothing sales. I know you'll play your part on our winning team."

At the end of the two-month training program Paulette was assigned a sales territory in Colorado under a new manager,

Cathie. In her first sales meeting the new Alaska parka was discussed. Cathie explained, "We have to decide if the high-end market is going to grow in the future and if being first would give us all a big advantage in this new, profitable market." Cathie had prepared several experienced reps in advance with sales figures. They gave examples of how profitable the future sales commissions could be if forecasts were right. A few reps disagreed initially and it took several hours of discussion until everyone had reached a consensus that the new parka offered the best opportunity for the future. At the end of the meeting Cathie recapped, "I'm happy everyone agreed that we'll concentrate on selling the new Alaska parka."

After the meeting Cathie told Paulette, "We operate this region just like a family. We're fair to everyone and treat them equally. We work hard to listen to everyone's opinions and their agreement with our team goals. This way we're all totally committed toward working together to be successful.

Charlie and Cathie represent clear examples of the authoritarian style and consensus style of decision-making. Your manager will probably tend toward one or the other.

MANAGING STYLE INDICATORS

One way to compare and determine how your manager expects decisions to be made — by either the authoritarian model or the consensus model — is to learn his definition of team or teamwork. Even though both Charlie and Cathie used the word "team," they meant very different things.

Charlie asked his team to follow instructions he gave as their coach. He gave them a decision and asked them to do their job quickly and efficiently, keeping objections quiet. The efficiency and speed with which the job gets done ensures success. Winning will be worth the sacrifice of commitment to the goal and hard work.

Cathie, on the other hand, defined her sales force differently. They were her "family." As facilitator of that family she treated each member as equal, asking for opinions, discussion and consensus. Taking the time to get everyone's agreement gave the team the commitment and motivation necessary to work together for the highest levels of success.

When you find out your boss's definition of "team" you will be on your way toward understanding a great deal about his managing style process.

UNDERSTANDING YOUR BOSS'S STYLE

Your boss's management style is important to you because the better you understand it — and are able to predict it — the better you can work with your boss to achieve common goals. Learning your boss's management style will take time. Don't expect it to come the first few months, but begin by observing and listening your very first day. The sooner you understand it the more effective you'll become.

Compare your boss's traits to the two stereotypes and determine which traits or combination of traits best fits him. Use the descriptions of the stereotypes to determine what areas your beliefs differ with your boss's. Determine what adjustments you will need to make so your boss will appreciate you. Concentrate on making those short-term adjustments and working within your boss's style. Remember, you will encounter people with different styles throughout your career. You will save yourself a lot of frustration if you learn to make adjustments in your style — no matter where your boss falls on the stereotype continuum.

WHAT IS YOUR MANAGING STYLE?

The first few years you will be learning about the managing style your boss uses. Observe other managers and teams as they make decisions in meetings you attend. Compare what you like and dislike about different managing styles and what you think would be the most effective for you.

You will see subtypes within the authoritarian and consensus models. Some managers will have a tendency to use one or a combination of the following: 1) fear and intimidation, 2) logic and reasoning, 3) emotion and instinct, 4) expertise and technical knowledge. Spend some time thinking about what process you prefer. In a few years you will be managing other people and you will influence — even control — the process. In later years you will have managers working for you and it will be necessary to evaluate their management styles. As you can see, the learning and understanding of managing style will be a career-long skill that will be critical to your success in business.

What Grads Should Know

IDENTIFY YOUR BOSS'S STYLE
  *If you learn the two managing stereotypes it will
    help you understand your boss's style.

DESCRIPTION OF MANAGEMENT STEREOTYPES
  *Authoritarian - decisions made by boss's individual
    judgement
  *Consensus - decisions made by group agreement

YOUR BOSS'S PREFERENCES
*The amount of discussion in meetings and length of meetings are good indicators of which stereotype is closest to your boss's style.

MANAGING STYLE INDICATORS
*Your boss's definition of "team" is a good indicator of managing style.

UNDERSTANDING YOUR BOSS'S STYLE
*If you understand your boss's style you can make the adjustments necessary to work better together.

WHAT IS YOUR MANAGING STYLE?
*In future years you will be managing other employees. What will be your style? Start now to analyze style.

Chapter 8

ORGANIZATION: FORMAL AND PERSONAL

Quick Reference:

- Formal Company Organization
    - Organizational Charts
    - Charting Your First Day
    - Organizational Chart Groups
    - Diagram - Formal Organizational Chart
- Personal Relationship Organization
    - Influence of Personal Relationships
    - Predicting Promotions
- What Grads Should Know

This chapter reveals the value of organizational charts. It will give you added insight into not only formal organization but also personal organization, and allow you to assess which employees will be able to help make your first promotion attainable. A working knowledge of your company's organizational chart is needed to understand who has authority within your company. Only then you understand how your company functions and who makes decisions.

FORMAL COMPANY ORGANIZATION

Organizational Charts

Try to start your first day (and company tour) with your company's organizational chart in hand. It will help you begin to understand the functions of your company. It will help you remember who you've met and who has authority. This will be valuable to you. It will help you understand the difference between "formal" organizational authority and personal influence.

As an example, let me impress upon you just how important your company's organization is. If I were hired by a new company and they could only FAX me two sheets of paper, I'd request the name, address and phone number of the person I was to report to on the first sheet, and the organizational chart on the second sheet.

The organizational chart is the basis for learning who works for the company, the purpose of their jobs, the relationships they have with each other and, in the simplest form possible, "how the company works."

To understand the people in your department, region or division you must first have an appreciation for their jobs: their titles and basic responsibilities, who they report to and which employees report to them. The most succinct way to digest this information is on the formal organizational chart. It makes no difference whether it is a small company with five employees or a large multi-national corporation with 400,000 employees. To understand who is in what job and how it relates to other jobs, you must understand the organizational chart.

You've received background in school about organizational charts. If not, pick up a basic management text and read the pertinent chapters. Throughout your career you'll find this chart to be a very valuable tool that will save you much time and spare you many mistakes.

Charting Your First Day

On the second day of the job, Harriet peeked into Doug's cubicle and asked him for a report she needed. She began by saying, "Hi, I'm Harriet, Mr. Johnson's secretary." Fortunately, Doug had taken a copy of his company's organizational chart on his tour the first day and had noticed S. Johnson was a senior vice president. Telling him who she worked for was all the authority this secretary needed to get Doug's attention and assistance. Had Doug been less aware he would have delayed her by checking with his manager to see if it was OK. Doug knew S. Johnson was his manager's boss. He didn't hesitate, gave her exactly what she wanted and was thanked later by his manager (for covering).

Power or no power? Will you jump or delay? What are your priorities? Take your company organizational chart on your first tour. If no formal, written chart is available ask the person giving you the tour to draw you a chart. You can fill in the names after meeting other employees. Start with your position and work your way to the top. Ask for help in diagraming this chart — specific to your company — and in filling in names.

After the first day, ask others you meet what their jobs are and who they report to. In this way you'll be able to fill in the details and complete your own chart. As it takes shape it will present a clearer picture — or description — of how the company works.

Organizational Chart Groups

Grads can be spared many mistakes by understanding "organizational chart groups" and how you can effectively relate to these groups. You can begin to understand what is expected of you from top senior managers to mail room clerks. You'll be prepared to interact more appropriately with everyone by noting: 1) who occupies which chart position, 2) their relationships with others, 3) characteristics of each job, and 4) how that job makes contact with you. Relating "more appropriately" means understanding where people fit into the organization, what traits they generally have in common and what interaction they expect to have with graduates. The following six organizational chart "groups" generalize common traits and suggest ways you can easily relate to these groups:
1) Senior Managers
2) Secretaries of Senior Managers
3) Middle Managers
4) Employees in Your Department
5) Secretaries
6) Administrative / Technical staff

SENIOR MANAGERS
Senior managers are normally in the forty- to sixty-year-old age range. Typically they'll be politically conservative. They've worked hard, are capable, successful and loyal to the company. Their interests revolve around other senior managers, stockholders and board members. They'll have little contact with you. If you want to meet them, go to your company's social functions. What you need to know about these senior managers is that if you say the wrong thing to them — whether at a casual retirement party, in an elevator, or at a company picnic — you are at risk of them not seeing you as senior

management potential. A word of caution: stick to the subjects of weather and sports in casual conversation with senior managers.

SECRETARIES OF SENIOR MANAGERS

Senior managers' secretaries derive all their power from their bosses and are typically very powerful. They may be any age, from twenty to sixty-five and are usually very capable, knowledgeable and experienced. Another word of caution: They may harbor some resentment toward a grad who has enjoyed the opportunity of a college education. You may be earning similar dollars, but you're fresh out of school and not yet "valuable" to anyone within the organization. They've proven themselves as loyal and capable employees. You can bet if the secretary's boss has the choice between losing a graduate or a secretary, the graduate will be in trouble. You cross these secretaries and your problems are immediately compounded. They have the power to make you look very good or very bad and they're to be respected. Your contact with them can be very significant. You might sit next to one of these employees in the lunch room, or they might need your help completing their normal duties.

MIDDLE MANAGERS

Middle managers, including first-line supervisors, have many of the same characteristics of senior managers, but with some exceptions. Be aware of their numbers — and especially their loyalties. Whether a director or plant superintendent, there will be many more of these middle managers than senior managers. You'll have many opportunities for contact with them as you work together. In working on projects for them, be sure you are familiar with both your subject and their opinions regarding the project. Listen, learn and proceed with caution.

"Primary internal loyalty" is one very important characteristic with management levels that you must be careful to observe. To whom are these middle managers loyal? First they consider themselves; second, their managers; then, senior managers; then other middle managers; and lastly, "other employees." You're in that group of "other employees." What this says to you is that you can't approach middle managers expecting their loyalty. Be careful what you say to whom, especially in this group. You can expect them to confide to your boss anything you've shared with them. This is the way their loyalties are defined. Show these managers the same respect that you show senior managers.

EMPLOYEES IN YOUR DEPARTMENT
Employees within your department are entirely different. Day-to-day contact, lunches, breaks and working together will create an atmosphere where you know them as well as you know your own family. Through sharing similar projects, functions and frustrations you'll find their help will be critical to getting your job done. You'll depend on each other. They comprise a cross-section of the population: varying ages, beliefs, backgrounds, education and philosophies of life. You'll develop close, personal relationships as you achieve common successes and failures. The most favorable working relationships need to be honest, friendly and sincere while staying business-oriented. Maintain your positive image by practicing your most important skill: creating positive relationships. Good, strong, close relationships with these department employees will be absolutely critical to your success.

SECRETARIES
Another work group is that of the remaining secretaries, managers' secretaries, administrative assistants and others who

do word processing and administrative duties for a specific person or persons (not the secretarial pool). The most important information you need to know about all secretaries is: who's their boss? Identify to whom each secretary reports. Although they have little formal authority, they have a great deal of personal influence. They deal with management on a daily basis. Expect these employees to be organized, efficient and knowledgeable about company procedures, rules and rumors. They have knowledge not only about how the company functions and what the rules are, but who follows the rules and who doesn't. They are privy to and knowledgeable about people within the organization, working relationships and personal relationships. You may find them to be less than supportive of you if you don't show proper respect to them and their positions. Treat all of them with the same care and respect you would give their bosses.

ADMINISTRATIVE - TECHNICAL STAFF
Administrative clerks and technicians comprise another work group. This group is below the level of first-line supervisor and includes computer operators, bookkeepers and other salaried employees. On an organizational chart they might report to a first-line supervisor or to a middle manager. They typically don't supervise staff (other than an occasional temporary or clerical employee). They live in the same world you live in. You'll probably have a lot of contact with this group. They're very knowledgeable in their own specialty and can be the most important people in the company in their specific disciplines. Taken for granted they can show the same lack of support as secretaries for what you're doing. It is recommended you pay careful attention to them because they'll be absolutely critical to you in your success if you need something in their specialty. These employees present a perfect opportunity

for you to practice your most important skill of developing positive relationships. You have the opportunity of regular contact with them and they're more experienced than you are. Any errors you make as you practice using your most important skill will impact your career less than when you begin using it on middle and senior managers. Be careful to show proper respect, especially if they are significantly older than you are.

Diagram of Formal Organizational Chart

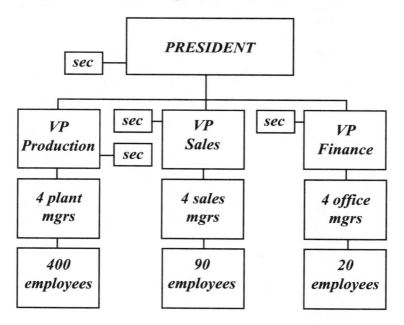

When we compare this abbreviated organizational chart to our six groups we find them located as follows:
1) Senior Managers - The president and three vice presidents.

2) Secretaries to Senior Managers - four secretaries of (1) above
3) Middle Managers - four plant managers, four sales managers, four office managers, plus managers not listed, i.e. eight production supervisors, eight sales managers, four accounting managers.
4) Department employees - department sizes range from four employees in cost accounting to 35 in the largest production department.
5) Secretaries - eighteen secretaries excluding four listed in (2) above.
6) Administrative / Technical - eight in office, ten in production, three in sales.

Included in this organizational chart are 420 production workers and 82 sales representatives that are not listed in the six groups above.

PERSONAL RELATIONSHIP ORGANIZATION (PRO)

What is a company's Personal Relationship Organization (PRO)? The PRO is the sum total of all the personal relationships among those people within the formal organization. These "personal relationships" are often unofficial, not being based on the formal authority of the structured organizational chart. These relationships might be based on friendships, working relationships, family and relatives, school or political affiliations, and/or any previous history together.

Why is it important for you to understand your company's PRO? Many times these personal relationships are stronger than the formal, organized relationships. Because these relationships are stronger, it's quite likely major decisions will be swayed — if not made — as a result of these relationships. Knowing the personal history of two people may allow you to position yourself so you can benefit from the relationship. You can benefit by the inevitable moves and changes which shape business. Knowing your company's PRO will help you identify key people who will eventually be able to affect your career. Get to know these people. Once you've identified them, then practice your most important skill: develop positive relationships with them. You may find you'll be able to "predict" promotions — yours and others — when you get very good at understanding 1) your company's "formal" organizational chart, and 2) its "informal" personal relationship organization, or PRO.

Influence of Personal Relationships

Predicting promotions is a very important part of learning a company's organization (formal or personal). A simple example can be made of the formal organizational chart listed above. The "unexpected" can be predicted with better accuracy by those who learn something about personal relationships.

Let's say the president, Max Sterling, plans to retire and become chairman of the board.   Looking at the chart again, notice the three key positions which report to our President: V.P. production (with 450 employees reporting), V.P. sales (with 90 employees reporting) and V.P. finance (with 20 employees reporting).   We can see that the V.P. in charge of production controls over 80% of the employees. We also know that a critical factor — manufacturing the product — is controlled by this V.P. He is in a very good position to be promoted. By knowing the company's formal organizational chart we can almost assume that he has the best chance to become the new president.

However, factor in the PRO and everything begins to shift. Knowledge of personal relationships would tell us that the V.P. of sales was hired in the Oklahoma sales district 25 years ago by Max Sterling. Both graduated from the same college (fraternal ties), have become good friends (close personal ties) and have come out of the sales side of the organization (valuing similar sales experience). They've grown to respect each other through all these shared experiences. They have formed a very strong informal personal relationship, in addition to their formal organizational chart positions. If it were up to Max to pick his own successor, he'd probably choose his friend, the V.P. of sales.

Besides this relationship, however, we additionally uncover a further complicating yet intriguing bit of information. One of the four production plant managers is the sister of Dan, the V.P. of Finance. Together they come from a very wealthy family. In fact, their family business was bought out by this company. Combined they now represent the second largest stockholder in the company. This personal and monetary relationship (based on ownership) is extremely powerful. Dan and his sister have a great deal of input into discussions about who will assume the presidency. In fact, Dan could now become the leading candidate for Max Sterling's job.

Predicting Promotions

If you knew only the formal organizational chart you'd believe the V.P. of Production to be the leading candidate. Having partial information about the V.P. of Sales you'd believe that person would be promoted. If you had only ownership information, you'd figure the V.P. of Finance to have it in the bag. With all the personal relationship information you've been able to uncover you're now in a position to predict the promotion with a much greater degree of accuracy. The information you acquire about your company's formal organization and personal relationships will help you understand the key people in your company and how decisions are made. It will help you predict the future. This information will be critical to you in various stages in your career.

Identifying key people may help you predict what effect they might have on your career. Once you identify these key people, use your most important skill to build a positive relationship with them.   As an example, if you're in the organization with Max as President and you know Max will be retiring, you would want to know that the V.P. of Sales and the V.P. of Finance are probably the two most likely candidates to become his successor. There may be openings in sales or finance based on who is moved up and who they pick as their successors. You may be able to position yourself for your own advancement.

Predicting promotions can be important the first year, even with all the habits you are trying to develop, the skills you are trying to learn, the new job you are trying to do and the new people you are meeting.

A good example of someone who listened but chose not to position herself would be Ann. Ann came into the accounting department right after college under Dan, the VP of Finance. There were two jobs open, one in the internal audit department and one in cost accounting. She was given her choice by the Controller. He explained that both he and the V.P. of Finance had come out of cost accounting. Cost accounting was considered very important to the organization, even though it was a smaller department on the organizational chart. Ann considered both jobs carefully. Recognizing the travel benefits in auditing she chose the auditing position. Another trainee was soon hired for the cost accounting department. Two years later when Dan, the V.P. of Finance, was in fact promoted to Max Sterling's job, the controller took Dan's job as V.P. of Finance. He then chose the cost accountant, not Ann, for his old controller's position. Ann was very disappointed that she hadn't been considered for the job. After thinking it over she realized both Dan and the Controller had told her the importance of cost accounting experience when she was hired. Both felt more comfortable having a controller with the same background they had found beneficial.

What Grads Should Know:

FORMAL ORGANIZATION
*Organizational Chart - Understand the value of an organizational chart in learning employees, their jobs, authority and reporting relationships within the formal organization.

CHARTING YOUR FIRST DAY
*Try to get an organizational chart to use your first day, or you can make up your own before and after meeting people.

ORGANIZATIONAL CHART GROUPS
*Learn common traits within each of the six employee groups and how grads should relate to each group.

DIAGRAM OF FORMAL ORGANIZATIONAL CHART
*Diagram of a manufacturing company, relating how the six "employee groups" fit in.

PERSONAL RELATIONSHIP ORGANIZATION (PRO)
*Unofficial personal relationships are based on friendships, favors, common dependence or positive relationships which link or bind employees together in ways other than the formal organization.

INFLUENCE OF PERSONAL RELATIONSHIPS
*They are often stronger than formal organizational chart authority.

PREDICTING PROMOTIONS
*If you have knowledge of both the formal and personal organizations you will be better able to make predictions and achieve your goals.

Chapter 9

POLITICS

Politics in business can harm your career if you don't understand it; but it can benefit your career if you know how others will practice it. Learn the five main political categories explained in this chapter as your first step in understanding politics and making sure your career will benefit from politics.

YOUR OPINION COUNTS

"Politics" Bad Rap

The word politic began as a Greek root with a generally positive meaning.   Webster,[1] defines politic as "having practical wisdom; prudent; shrewd; diplomatic."   Second and third definitions define its more recent, popular connotation: "2) Crafty; unscrupulous, 3) prudently or artfully contrived; expedient, as a plan, action, remark, etc. . . ." Politics is a word you will hear many times throughout your business career. Understanding its positive and negative use by employees you work with will help you in your career.

Negative Opinions

Politics is important because it will be used to explain many promotions or advantages one employee achieves over another. It will often be used negatively by those employees who feel taken advantage of or who didn't get a hoped-for promotion. As a primarily negative term, "politics" will most often be used by employees who lack confidence in their personal relationship skills.   They very often feel they've been harmed by actions which they judge as unfair or selfish.   Additionally, they recognize they have not met their career goals and blame others for their inadequacies.

Employees with a negative opinion of politics will use descriptions such as "He's too political," or "She's always playing politics," or "He's a political animal."

---

[1] *Webster's New World Dictionary,* William Collins+World Publishing Co., Inc.

Positive Opinions

In contrast, employees who have a positive opinion of politics rarely even use the word "politics."

Employees with a positive opinion are those who have confidence in their personal relationship skills. They've had success in developing positive relationships and in using these relationships to achieve their goals. They have probably benefited from interdependent relationships with other employees. These employees tend to be positive about their career progress.

Because the word "politics" has a wide-spread, negative connotation these employees usually use terms like "personal relationship skills," or "people skills," or "interpersonal skills" to describe the same actions that negative people call "politics."

FIVE POLITICAL CATEGORIES

To develop a positive opinion of politics and use it to benefit your career you should learn to recognize employees political attitudes. Attitudes can be recognized by learning the political similarities each group has in common. There are five main political categories based on attitudes.

Category   Political Attitude

1) NAIVELY INNOCENT. . Politics doesn't exist

2) IDEALIST. . . . . Politics is the use of unfair relationships and must be eliminated.

3) DISGRUNTLED LOSER. Politics is the use of unethical relationships that harm honest people

4) ACHIEVER. . . . . Politics is the use of positive relationships that help achieve your goals.

5) POWER SEEKER. . . . . . Politics is the use of any relationship that gets you to the top

Description Of Categories

1) NAIVELY INNOCENT

The Naively Innocent believes politics doesn't exist and that both personal relationships and friendships are put aside and ignored when managers make advancement decisions. The Naively Innocent likes to think that everyone is always unselfish, sincere and that comments about "playing politics" or "good old boy favoritism" are untrue. This type of employee prefers to treat all employees equally and doesn't understand the need for politically sensitive treatment of higher management. The lack of political instincts can cause problems when dealing with powerful employees.

Grads should be very careful in dealing with the Naively Innocent because his lack of political awareness can make the grad look disloyal or incompetent. Kyland found out the kind of problems a Naively Innocent employee can cause when failing to be sensitive toward higher management.

Brendan, Kyland's boss, stormed into Kyland's office, "You're going to have to get rid of that kid — that clerk Steve — in the front office."

Kyland set aside the material on his desk to give Brendan his undivided attention. "What's he done?"

"He answered the phone this morning and told Chris — our Vice President Chris — that I was out playing golf. Why in the world would he tell a vice president I'm out playing golf? All he had to say was that I was out of the office until noon. How did he find out I was out playing golf anyway?"

Kyland avoided the question, addressing the larger issue, "I'll talk to him and make sure it won't happen again. I'm really sorry, Brendan." But Brendan was already out the door, still mumbling.

Kyland hesitated a moment, thinking how he'd say this diplomatically. He then picked up the phone to ask Steve to come into his office. He'd have to try and make Steve aware of the consequences of saying the wrong thing to an important person within the company. Steve had just been naive. Kyland would have to be careful what he told Steve in the future; he couldn't rely on his political instincts.

2) IDEALIST

The Idealist believes personal goals must only be achieved by merit through job performance. Any type of "playing politics" is unfair. All promotions should be based on actual measured achievement and gauged fairly and honestly. The Idealist will avoid any hint of politics when dealing with other employees, doing what he believes to be "right." The Idealist tends to be unconcerned whether the right employees are friends or enemies and believes people who play politics are brown-nosers and back-stabbers. He believes any type of politics will fail in the long run.

Because of his inflexibility the Idealist usually has problems as a manager. But he tends to be successful in specialty jobs not requiring the skill of managing people.

Grads should be careful about being associated with Idealists because they often have reputations of NOT being team players. They are often perceived as "rebels" in an organization. Kyland's instincts kept him out of trouble even on his first job.

One afternoon, Kyland and Mike, another employee and golfer he'd recently met, agreed to meet for a round of golf. Mike criticized the employees they knew in common; he appeared to have a rigid cut-and-dried philosophy about how he felt things should be. Nearing the ninth hole Mike became openly critical of Kyland's boss: "He spends all his time walking around chatting with the big boys. I wonder when he has time to do his job."

Kyland was disturbed. Not at what Mike had said, it was true that his boss spent a lot of time with upper management. Kyland was concerned with Mike's open, negative criticism. He'd always been taught that being openly critical of a boss spelled big trouble: trouble for the guy expressing the criticism.

Kyland kept his opinion to himself until the next day. Still troubled, he confided in Janet, a friend who had several years of experience with his new company. She confirmed his discomfort: "Mike's mouth is his own worst enemy. He's offended just about everybody at one time or another. He may be good at his job, but he can't deal with people. I don't think they'll ever let him manage anyone. My advice is to stay away from that one. You'll get painted with the same brush." Kyland didn't initiate any more golf with Mike and found other, more positive golfers for his Saturday or Sunday games. He was glad he had chosen to steer clear when he saw the reputation Mike had developed for himself.

3) DISGRUNTLED LOSER
The Disgruntled Loser, you can bet, has lost at least one promotion or career objective to another employee. The other

employee was probably more qualified, but rather than admit someone could be better, this Loser blames his misfortune on politics. After all, he reasons, it's company politics which is the basis for most decisions and he, the Loser, believes strongly that this good-old-boy-network of back-scratching and gamesmanship only takes advantage of the hardworking, ethical employees. In fact, this very employee is often self-righteous and the most negative toward politics. It is the Disgruntled Loser who often projects his negative attitude onto managers or anyone in authority.

Grads should avoid being associated with these employees. Kyland had already experienced the Naively Innocent, and more recently the Idealist. He was just about to run into this third type: Fred, the Disgruntled Loser.

Because one of Kyland's customers was refused credit for late payment, Kyland made a personal visit to the accounting department where he spoke with Fred, a longtime accountant with the company. "Fred, the manager at my account knows they've been late but has agreed to a solution to speed up payments. Let's work with them on this; it's just been a tough six months for their industry."

Fred gave Kyland no eye contact but, moving his pen as if to write, said with finality, "I don't have time to call every delinquent account. If they've got a payment plan tell 'em to put it in writing. When — and if — they do I'll release the credit hold."

Kyland felt Fred's request was unreasonable. Customers have choices to buy elsewhere; they shouldn't have to write letters. After considering the alternatives Kyland went to Brendan, who confirmed Fred's negative attitude. "Fred has always been inflexible and has poor people skills; that's why he wasn't promoted to credit manager. He's gotten worse since he was passed over. We can't ask customers to write us letters about their payment plans! Leave this with me, I'll take care of it."

Kyland was glad to leave it alone. The next day Kyland learned that Fred had, indeed, called his customer and released the credit hold. He was impressed at how Brendan was able to get things accomplished. Additionally he found out via the grapevine that Fred had been given a warning about his job performance. Two months later Kyland was surprised (but not at all disappointed) to learn that Fred had left the company. Kyland had learned a lot about people with negative opinions about politics. He made a conscious note to take extra care around employees with very negative attitudes.

4) THE ACHIEVER

The Achiever's primary concern is to achieve personal career goals through positive relationships. He realizes the necessity of political relationships in expediting his work, and the importance of these relationships in being able to be "the best" and to have a successful career.

The Achiever has a pro-active opinion of politics and doesn't hesitate to use political relationships to achieve his goals. He believes in a long-term political attitude that avoids enemies and tries to make every situation a win/win one, benefiting himself as well as other employees. The Achiever uses his most important skill (chapter 2) to develop these positive, long-term relationships.

Many successful managers are in this category. Advancement prospects are good for the Achiever. He will rarely lose his job because he has support from all levels of management. The combination of positive relationships and lack of enemies permits steady growth.

Grads should learn political skills from the Achiever and consider making the Achiever's attitude their personal political attitude.

Kyland had always assumed his boss, Brendan, would fall into the Achiever category. Brendan had a reputation of being very good at his job as National Sales Manager. Kyland had never felt comfortable enough to ask him about his political attitude. Late one night on a return flight after a successful contract negotiation, Brendan brought up the subject.

"Kyland, to tell you the truth I worked harder and was better than anyone else. That's what it boils down to. I put in longer hours and got noticed for producing. I made it my personal standard to always be the best, I was recognized for it and got promoted. This promotion culminates 15 years of planned success. It's really based on three accomplishments. First, I was the best at every job I had. Second, I was successful in all four areas required to be a national sales manager: district sales, regional sales, product development, and marketing management. And last, and most important, is that I developed good relationships with all decision makers along the way to getting each promotion — from the first as District Sales Manager — to the last as National Sales Manager

I spent a great deal of my time developing positive relationships with employees at every level. I even postponed some of my personal goals to make sure the right people also benefitted as I took the long-term approach. I kept thinking that sooner or later these strong relationships would help me get ahead."

Kyland was surprised by Brendan's directness and all the hard work it had taken to benefit from positive political relationships.

Sensing Kyland's surprise, Brendan continued, "You've only seen the last year when I've been concentrating on developing senior management relationships. Actually these relationships have been the most important part of a fifteen-year career process. That's why some people think all I've been doing is playing politics with the big boys."   Kyland was startled, recognizing Mike's exact words on the golf course.

Kyland began to realize there was a lot more planning, dedication and hard work involved to accomplish the career goal of "developing positive relationships" than what he'd originally thought.

5) THE POWER SEEKER

The Power Seeker has a constant drive to win at all costs. They are willing to harm or even destroy other employees' careers to achieve or maintain personal goals, this type of employee is to be watched and steered away from.   They create enemies without concern and won't hesitate to use fear to control and intimidate others. They often either attain a top position within their companies or are forced to leave by their enemies. These Power Seekers have a very low ethical concern for the rights of others.   People in this category commit most of the actions that tend to harm others and they are cited as negative examples of being "political" by those who hold a negative opinion about office politics.

Grads should be quick to identify Power Seekers and exercise caution in dealing with them. Kyland had been warned previously.   It shouldn't have been any surprise the day it happened.

Lynn, a regional manager in charge of eight stores, called Kyland to double her normal order. She also wanted the order shipped on a rush basis for a big promotional sale. Kyland was excited. These figures would really make his month look good — and she'd called him and not his boss, Brendan.

Kyland was to have lunch with Brendan and told him about the order. But instead of being pleased, Brendan appeared upset, warning Kyland, "Don't do anything with Lynn until we talk. She purposely ordered through you to avoid the company rule.

Her order is against our company policy; she's trying to load up her region to get top volume region for the year. If she gets caught she'll say she was given the OK by Brendan's department, making it my fault. I've seen her try to do this type of thing before. She's super competitive and doesn't care who she hurts to get ahead."

Kyland could hardly believe a manager at her level would intentionally set out to hurt their department. Kyland's lesson from Lynn was to pay more attention to people's reputations and intentions. Only then would he have a better understanding of who he could trust and who he needed to watch out for.

LEARNING ABOUT POLITICS

But why is it important to learn about the categories? Recognizing what category or political attitude another employee falls into will start to develop the grad's awareness of opinions and attitudes about politics which will help or hinder his career.

Not everyone you meet will fit neatly into one of the five categories. But try to understand their personal motivations, opinions of politics, methods of developing relationships and achieving personal goals. Understanding their underlying attitudes will give you a head start by giving you a clearer picture and advantage over others who don't understand positive politics. Politics can be fun: predict and avoid being in the wrong place at the wrong time. Judge correctly and be in exactly the right place at the right time; that's how to use your knowledge to help achieve your own career goals.

It was within a few short months that Kyland had the first big test of his ability to assess and act on political opinions and attitudes. Brendan put him in charge of a project to plan a sales meeting along with two other employees, Catherine and Dietrich.

When giving Kyland the project, Brendan explained that Catherine and Dietrich had volunteered for the assignment. Dietrich had asked to manage it; Catherine wanted to do the winter negotiations with the vendors in Florida.

It was Kyland's call as far as assigning duties and he didn't want Dietrich to get all the credit with management. He was learning quickly from Brendan and saw this as a political opportunity to get some personal recognition: hurting no one, but making sure that he was the one in the right place at the right time.

Kyland determined that Dietrich was a Power Seeker and after as much recognition as he could get. Catherine was very close to a Naively Innocent and had no negotiating experience. He wanted to give them what they wanted, but elected to meet with them individually before assigning duties. After their individual conversations, Kyland decided to assign the negotiation jobs to Dietrich, the internal record keeping and printing jobs to Catherine, and he would handle all management contact jobs himself.

Looking back after the meeting, Kyland congratulated Dietrich on his aggressiveness, which had gotten good prices from the vendors. Catherine's lack of awareness hadn't been a problem with the internal duties he'd given her, and he thanked her for a job well done. But best of all, Kyland was able to get good management exposure and credit for managing a successful project. He was satisfied with the changes he'd undergone. Just one year ago he would have acquiesced and handed all the management exposure jobs to Dietrich. He had learned a lot by watching Brendan and thinking about others' political motivations.

What Grads Should Know

YOUR OPINION COUNTS
   *Negative Opinions
      Employees with limited personal relationship
      skills or who have had career problems usually
      have negative opinions of politics

   *Positive Opinions
      Employees with good relationship skills and
      successful careers have positive opinions of
      politics.

FIVE POLITICAL CATEGORIES
   *Grads should learn to recognize these categories to
      understand employees' political strengths and
      weaknesses.

      1) Naively Innocent - "Politics" doesn't exist; all
      personal relationships are ignored when career
      advancement decisions are made.

      2) Idealist - All "politics" is unfair, all career
      advancement should be made strictly on job
      performance, not personal relationships

      3) Disgruntled Loser - "Unethical politics" has
      caused their careers harm; decisions are made
      within dishonest political relationships.

4) Achiever - "Politics" boils down to the natural people skills of building relationships, with all decisions directly affected by relationships.

5) Power Seeker - "Politics" is just competitive human nature; obsession to be on top at any price, even if harm should come to others.

LEARNING ABOUT POLITICS
*To start understanding politics and employees' political motivations, learn to recognize these five categories. Identifying them will help a grad predict potential actions which will undoubtedly affect — and might very well benefit — his career.

Chapter 10

HIGH VISIBILITY SITUATIONS

Quick Reference

- Unique Opportunities
- Meetings
- Social and Business Events
- Business Lunches
- Business Travel
- Public Speaking
- Situations as Opportunities
- What Grads Should Know

A successful career may depend upon how you are perceived in highly visible situations, whether they be meetings or lunches, while traveling or speaking, or in any social business settings. Sometimes more important than what you do is what you avoid doing. This chapter prepares you to gradually improve your performance during high visibility situations and encourages you to use these tips to your advantage.

UNIQUE OPPORTUNITIES

High visibility situations are unique opportunities to meet others and to become known. Since your "most important skill" is to develop positive working relationships, these opportunities to meet and get to know others are tremendously beneficial to your career.

Your primary contact with managers (those who make the final decisions on promotions) will probably be during one of these high visibility situations. Appreciate and take advantage of each situation; do not miss any opportunity.

MEETINGS

Meetings are opportunities for exposure and visibility. Be careful what you say and do because the impression you give during these meetings will be important. The type of business meeting matters because expectations are different depending upon the type of meeting. There is a great deal to be learned by knowing in advance the type of meeting you are expected to attend.

Are you only to visit and say nothing or are you expected to present information? It is wise to remember two general meeting rules. When in doubt, always 1) keep it brief, and 2) check with your manager before you offer input.

Types of Meetings

WORKING MEETING
The purpose of this type of meeting is to gather ideas or to accomplish a common goal. It's generally attended by mid-level managers or below. The atmosphere is very informal and

participants are encouraged to offer their ideas and work together. The purpose of a working meeting is not to make a final decision, but to prepare a memo or to establish a project as a basis for a decision to be made at a later date.

Research what the meeting is to accomplish. The agenda centers around the project that needs to be completed. Your input can be valuable.

DECISION MEETING
The purpose of this type of meeting is to make decisions on a number of pre-determined agenda items. These meetings will be strictly controlled by the person presiding; for instance, in board meetings the chairman will lead the meetings. Decision meetings have two types of participants: the presenters and the decision-makers.

If you attend one of these meetings within your first year of employment, it will probably be either in the capacity of presenter or to receive an education by watching those giving presentations.

REGULAR STAFF OR UPDATE MEETING
The purpose of this regularly scheduled meeting is to allow everyone within a department to update the manager and other members of the group on the status of each area of responsibility.

Always follow the two important rules regarding regular update meetings: 1) keep it brief and, 2) check everything you intend to say with your manager before the meeting.

INTRODUCTION MEETING
The purpose of this type of meeting is to introduce employees to someone or to introduce employees to each other. A brief history is given of each employee's time with the company along with a brief explanation of her major area of responsibility.

If you are asked to prepare anything for one of these meetings be sure to keep it brief and check with your boss before attending to ensure that what you are going to say is appropriate.

Preparing For Meetings

Prior to any meeting find out the type of meeting and purpose. Get a copy of the agenda. Who is scheduled to attend? Identify the relationships between those attending by consulting your organizational chart (Organization: Formal and Personal, chapter 8). Find out what is expected to happen. Lastly, determine what is expected from you.

ARRIVE AT MEETING
Always be five minutes early to meetings and use this time to meet people you don't know. Don't sit down until someone invites you to sit down and indicates where they would like you to sit. This is important, as you don't want to sit in the boss's chair. You will learn a lot if you listen carefully. When you talk let it be safe, small talk: weather, sports or current events.

DURING THE MEETING
Sketch a seating chart, casually. Note each participant's location and name. Keep your notes brief; use the agenda to record your notes. Too many notes will make you look like a secretary. One of the best rules is to remain silent until you get to know what is going on.

If you don't know someone in the meeting, find out their name immediately after the meeting and fill it in on your seating chart, noting their participation.

AFTER THE MEETING

Discuss the meeting with another person from your department who also attended. Casually, before or after work, ask them what really happened. This may seem like a strange request, but someone who knows the company and the participants may see the interaction from a different perspective than what a newcomer is able to notice. In Sid's case he didn't have long to wait before Alex, his supervisor, asked him to observe a company meeting. He would later be surprised by Alex's interpretation.

Alex asked Sid to sit in a chair along the wall. "Just watch what happens and we'll go to lunch afterwards to discuss it." That was just before a confrontation began during the meeting. Ordering sandwiches an hour later, Sid told Alex about the marketing manager, Jeff's, open disagreement with the president. "I was surprised. Is there a problem between those two?" Alex smiled and leaned back, "You were right to be surprised; it was an unusual public confrontation. I thought you'd enjoy it. Some background you don't know is that he and the president are very good friends. Jeff is smart enough to have had that disagreement first in private. What you witnessed was actually for the benefit of the marketing department. They feel very strongly about the new ads and Jeff had to publicly support them. It was also important that the president publicly show he wouldn't change his mind and that the marketing department would be wasting their time trying to get new ads." Alex looked Sid squarely in the eye and added, "Our conversation won't go any further than the two of us, I presume."

Sid was starting to realize that he'd have to know the history and personal relationships of those involved to fully understand what was really happening within his new company. Back at the office he used his roughly-sketched seating chart to make sure he'd remember the names of each person at the meeting.

He updated his organizational chart, too, which would help him in the future to understand his company's informal organization. The interrelationships were becoming more and more interesting.

SOCIAL AND BUSINESS EVENTS

Social and business events include the formal Christmas party, the casual company picnic, or the get-together in the hospitality suite at a convention. It might be a gathering which honors others, like a retirement or service award dinner. Each offers a tremendous opportunity to meet other employees and for others to meet you. Your participation the first year or so will probably be limited only to those times when all employees are invited.

There are several rules that will enable you to enjoy social business events. These high visibility situations need be neither frightening nor embarrassing if you follow a few guidelines.

*The first rule for social functions is to ALWAYS attend. When you are invited do not avoid the chance to meet others and make a positive impression.

*The second rule is to treat these occasions with the same professional business image which you maintain at work. Dress, look and act as management. Remember you are always being judged as a business person no matter how social the event. Assume that everything you say — or that others say to you — will get directly back to your manager, even if she does not attend. Say nothing that could be easily misunderstood. Be friendly, gregarious and happy. Keep conversations light; remember: sports, weather or current events.

*The third rule is to maintain or develop manners. If your parents were always correcting your manners as you grew up

— both your table manners and your manners in introducing people to each other — your manners are probably fine for business. If manners weren't important in your family then your manners are probably not polished. Get hold of *Letitia Baldrige's Complete Guide to Executive Manners.*[2] Also ask a parent, professor or friend to help you polish your skills.

*Rule number four: keep drinking to a minimum. As a general rule, it is important to recognize that excessive drinking is considered to show a lack of personal discipline. Employees who drink too much do not have management potential. The safest approach is to have one drink last all night. Better yet, drink Sprite™ or ginger ale on the rocks.

*Rule number five is to mingle. Remember, this is an opportunity to meet people. Don't spend all your time, or even most of your time, with one person. If you're shy force yourself to meet people. When Sid attended his first holiday party it was a stretch. He felt uncomfortable at having to watch his own behavior so carefully. Going with Beth made it easier for him.

Sid was not looking forward to the Christmas party, but knew it was important for his career that he attend. Beth, another grad he'd met during training, had agreed to go with him. The decorations were impressive — if not intimidating — with the laser show, new marketing video and musicians already performing.

Beth ordered white wine, which he knew she'd sip all night; he ordered ginger ale with a twist. Gracefully maneuvering, they both managed to talk with three or four people before locating their table. Sid's goal was to talk with at least ten people, meeting at least five employees ranked above him he'd

---

[2] Letitia Baldridge's *Complete Guide to Executive Manners,* Edited by Sandi Gelles-Cole, Rawson Associates, 1985.

not known before. He knew the practice he got while introducing Beth would give him confidence (age to youth, women to men, greater status to lesser — he knew the guidelines). He'd armed himself for safe social talk by reading the latest trade publication, the latest Newsweek *and had scanned the local newspaper all month for local community news affecting other employees and their families. Social talk was becoming easier for him now that he knew the safe parameters. Beth's table manners were great so he enjoyed these functions when he could take her lead. His family had rarely eaten together and he knew his table manners had suffered.*

By eleven o'clock Sid had met five new people, and had talked with over a dozen he'd met before. Beth had been instrumental in introducing him to as many new faces as he had introduced to her. They both felt satisfied in their highly visible opportunity of meeting and getting to know people they wouldn't have contact with during work.

BUSINESS LUNCHES

Business lunches are a combination of a social occasion and a business meeting. Nearly everything already said about both social occasions and business meetings applies to the business lunch.

A business lunch is a meeting. The purpose of the lunch, your preparation before, the way you conduct yourself during, and how you analyze what has happened after the business lunch is identical to the business meeting with one exception. Do not draw a seating chart. Remember, do not sit down until someone tells you where to sit. Your social business image is essentially the same professional business image you project at other social occasions.

Business lunches will probably be limited to once a week or once a month the first year or two. Some will require very little, if any, preparation as with the get acquainted lunches. Some will require a great deal of preparation and much will depend on the outcome, as with the marketing lunch Alex asked Sid to attend.

Calling Sid into his office Alex closed the door. "Sid, I have scheduled an important lunch with marketing on Friday and because you understand how important it is to know the history of a situation in advance, I want to explain what it's all about. This one is different than the other two lunches we've had during your three months here. It's a continuation of the problem you heard discussed in the board room meeting. Marketing wants our department to pay for $20,000 of advertising out of our budget and I'm trying to diplomatically avoid it. I think I have convinced them to accept our help selling listings rather than the $20,000 they want. This gets me to the purpose of this lunch."

"I've offered marketing your help selling ads for two months. This will be a great opportunity for you to get sales experience within the company. But first we have to convince them of your sales ability. Here's the plan: during lunch I'll give a brief history of your summer job and sales exposure. I want you to give them some examples of selling to business and statistics on your overall sales results. Let's meet on Thursday to go over what you'll say."

On Thursday Sid went over his intended comments and on Friday the lunch went very well. Marketing was thrilled to have Sid and wanted him to start as soon as possible. After lunch and back at his office, Alex turned to Sid, "Good job with your facts and presentation. You just passed your first test on internal diplomacy."

BUSINESS TRAVEL

As a general rule, grads will not be required to do much business travel their first year or two. Exceptions to this are those jobs where primary duties are performed at customer locations such as with sales or customer service. If you are required to travel on business, make sure you project the same professional image as during work hours at your office. Also, treat all after-hours situations as business social events that your boss will hear about — even the most casual occasion with employees or customers.

The reality of business travel is that it is demanding and stressful. Most grads make the mistake of thinking business travel can be likened to vacationing. It can't. Most experienced employees avoid travel unless it is absolutely necessary. There is an old adage, "The only people who like to travel on business are people who haven't done it." Don't make the mistake many grads make: joking about missing all the fun of travel. It shows you really don't understand what business travel is like. If it is necessary for you to travel on your job it will be expressed as a percentage of time; 50% is very heavy travel requiring you to be gone half of your working days. Travel of 10% is considered light to moderate.

If you work for a company with several facilities, you may be asked to visit other locations to become familiar with different operations. If you are asked to travel take it seriously and treat it as a high visibility situation. Prepare diligently and make a good summary report to your boss upon your return.

PUBLIC SPEAKING

Public speaking will be a part of any successful business career. It will become more important the higher up you move within your company. You may not be asked to speak publicly within the first six months. However, it is never too early to begin observing what makes an effective speaker and to begin practicing the skills which will ultimately make you a polished speaker.

Almost all managers value public speaking ability as an indication of future management potential. Speaking in front of a group is a natural position of authority and leadership. Listeners assume that speaking skills indicate ability to motivate, influence and persuade others. There is also an assumption that a good speaker is intelligent, organized and articulate. These are all important management skills and why managers are favorably impressed by a graduate's speaking ability.

Seek opportunities to speak which will give you practice speaking. Join a public speaking organization such as *Toastmasters* to gain the practice you need. Everyone is nervous when they speak. How you learn to hide it — or control it — is the advantage of practice.

Some guidelines that will help you:

*First, be sure you are adequately prepared. Prepare in advance, know your subject forward and backward.

*Second, practice your speech many times before ever trying to address an audience you don't know. Then practice answering questions you feel might be asked.

*Third, know your audience. The better you know your audience and their familiarity with the subject on which you are speaking, the better prepared you can be for fielding questions.

*Fourth, be careful with humor. Don't use it unless you're sure it's appropriate and clean.

*Last, be sure you review the speech with your manager— just the key points — so she knows in advance what you are preparing to say.

SITUATIONS AS OPPORTUNITIES

Whatever high visibility situation you are given, it is an opportunity that can never be duplicated and one that should not be missed. Some graduates don't realize the importance of meetings, lunches and social situations. Use these opportunities to start forming positive relationships and the time you spend will reward you.

What Grads Should Know:

HIGH VISIBILITY SITUATIONS
*These situations are unique opportunities to make contacts, start developing positive relationships and to present a professional business image.

MEETINGS
*If you know the purpose of a meeting you can better participate and create a professional image.
*Remember the four types of meetings:
- Working
- Decision
- Staff or Update
- Introduction
*Know your role in each type.

SOCIAL AND BUSINESS EVENTS
*Practice the five rules of social/business events:
- Always attend
- Maintain professional image
- Use good manners
- Limited alcohol and
- Mingle; concentrate on meeting managers you
don't know.

BUSINESS LUNCHES
*Learn the purpose of lunch in advance and your
role in it.
*Practice your five social business rules.

PUBLIC SPEAKING
*Start practicing now; it will become more important
as your career progresses.
*Use suggestions to improve your speaking skills.

Chapter 11

TEAM DUTIES

Teamwork is one of the most important and most critical elements in achieving a successful business career. It's not just working together, but working together as interdependent teams, recognizing multi-level goals that will bring you the most success. This chapter deals with the rules and exceptions to the rules that make teamwork enjoyable.

BASIS OF ORGANIZATION

The success of any organization is dependent upon all team members, just like winning a football game depends not on one player but on the entire team. There may be a star player who gets all the attention, but for a team to be successful all team members must perform their individual duties. Teamwork is the basis of success not just for business, but for all organizations including government, schools, churches and the military. Working together works and "not working together" doesn't work. The success of teamwork shows up most noticeably in the business world where competition is more intense.

MORE IMPORTANT IN BUSINESS

Teamwork is important in any organization. As an example, in schools there are teams working to provide an education to students. Your university team was composed of professors, administrators, recruiters and alumni.

In businesses, teamwork is even more important than in other organizations. Because of the intense competition in the private sector, teamwork is not only the basis of business success but also of business survival. If a business team fails to work together to service its customers at a reasonable price, competitors will take away those customers and the company will go out of business. If team members cannot work together, businesses can change quickly as Josh found out in his summer job.

Josh lived in North Carolina and had two uncles in the furniture business. After his third year at college he returned to help them at their small furniture factory. Ben was older, bolder and bright. Chris was young, relaxed and chatty. Both were arguing his very first day about which customers to concentrate their sales efforts on; Ben wanting to sell through wholesale distributors, Chris wanting to sell direct to furniture chains. As the summer progressed the disagreement continued. Ben and Chris each decided to sell to the customers they preferred. Sales were good, in fact very good, and the factory began to fall behind in its delivery schedules. More factory workers were hired but quality began to decrease. The two brothers continued to argue about whose orders took priority; production was further increased. By September, when Josh began his senior year, two orders had been returned due to quality control issues. By Christmas, Josh returned to find their three largest wholesale customers had switched to another furniture maker. Josh couldn't believe that his two uncles would ruin their successful business because of an unresolved disagreement and refusal to work as a team to be successful. By the next year Ben demanded that his brother buy him out. Two years later Chris was forced to sell the business altogether and Ben was working for a competitor. How quickly even a family business had deteriorated when key members were unable to work together as a team to achieve a common goal.

MULTI-LEVEL TEAMS

The heart of any business, large or small, is composed of one or more teams of employees working together to achieve common goals. In a small company of five employees, all five make up a team that works together. In a large company of 100,000, each individual department may have two to 25 employees working together as a team on one function. Each of these individual departments together will also make up another team which works together to produce a product in a plant. All plants make up still another team that will ultimately achieve the goal of the company. Now we're talking about multi-level teams.

Most graduates will work in companies where they are members of more than one of these multi-level teams at a time. Holding a broad understanding and seeing the "big picture" will guarantee that many different goals can exist at the same time. Occasionally they appear to conflict. Having the company's long-term interests at heart will allow resolutions to these apparent conflicts. This is what Josh found out in his first job as supervisor for a 500-employee furniture manufacturer.

His summer job experience with his uncles enabled Josh to start out as a supervisor and his primary team of seven carpenters had 180 wooden kitchen chairs to assemble as their daily goal. These would accompany the kitchen tables produced by Frank Anderson's team. Josh's primary team was one of four teams within the plant producing matching table and chair sets. The chairs had to match the tables in grade of wood, size, shape and stain to allow them to be sold most profitably in sets rather than as singles.

Sometime into his fourth month Frank asked to have lunch with Josh. As they talked, Josh learned that over 5% of his chairs required adjustments in order to pair them with the tables produced by Frank's team. Frank helped Josh understand he was a member of not just one team, but three teams: 1) Josh and the seven carpenters, 2) the 75 employees in the kitchen furniture plant with the goal of making and matching kitchen sets, and 3) the team of 500 total companywide employees with a goal of profitably selling furniture to meet customers' needs.

Although Josh's primary team was meeting their goals of assembling their 180 chairs daily, his secondary team (the team of seventy-five in the plant) was falling behind, re-staining or restyling the chairs he sent them to match. This in turn undermined their ability to meet their team goals. This domino effect lessened the profitability of the entire company (his third team of 500 workers). Josh learned that profitability often meant balancing the conflicting demands made between his department's goals and the broader goals of his plant and company.

Understanding his company and the many teams of which he was a part gave Josh the bigger picture that enabled him to become an excellent team player. Josh found himself pleasing management by balancing company goals with his department's goals.

TEAM DEPENDENCY

For the team to achieve its goals team members must depend on each other to complete their projects on or before deadline. Many times one team cannot start until another team has completed their job.

Take the airline industry as an example. Within one company is reservations, flight service, maintenance, baggage handling, cargo, etc. In order for you to book a flight and get from point A to point B you need a timely reservation and ticket in hand — reservations must do their job. You arrive at the airport, ticketing checks you in and sends your bags to the baggage handlers in a timely fashion. Both bags and passenger arrive at the gate and the gate agent verifies you as the passenger while the baggage handlers load your luggage. The flight crew prepares the aircraft and flies you to your destination. All work together to ensure a flawless flight. Each employee is not only part of the department team, but part of a larger team (passenger coordination or baggage/cargo handling) and the largest team (the entire company).

Most graduates understand team dependency on the basis of function, such as the airline ticket agent issuing the ticket and baggage being loaded into the plane. But many graduates don't realize the urgency of deadlines. In school many deadlines were individual and flexible: if a class was not completed on time you could take an incomplete and finish it later. In business, deadlines are team-dependent. They are much more critical when you understand your membership in multi-level teams. In the airline industry the ticket agents have hourly deadlines to get tickets issued within their team of agents. They also must be aware of changing deadlines when flights are delayed or canceled by the larger team (including flight crews, mechanics or cargo). Deadlines are much more critical in business and successful graduates understand their multi-level team responsibility.

TERRITORIAL CONTROL

Territorial control is a possessiveness of one's own immediate personal or team goals. It is a function of overcontrolling and often hinders teamwork. By not focusing on the larger teams of which one is a part, this type of control restricts teamwork by narrowly focusing on one's own small department. It does not see the advantage of the whole business function as a team and lessens the company's ability to be profitable by not allowing all parts to work together as a fully functioning unit.

Territorial control is usually practiced by more experienced employees who have been part of a department for a long time. They make the goals of their team their own. Yet they have carried it one step too far and have lost the ability to see the larger picture of which they are a part.

Grads should expect to encounter occasional bouts of territorial control, to observe it when noticed, and to guard against ever practicing it. Territorial control prevents teams from working together. *That's what Josh found out when Chad, a long-time carpenter in his department, explained that some of the braces were too large to fit into the chair legs. The large braces had to be taken back to the lathe department and a carpenter had to wait until a lathe operator could interrupt his work and run the braces through the sander. Chad suggested that some carpenters could be taught to use the sander in the lathe department so they wouldn't have to wait for an operator. Josh approached the Lathe Supervisor, Max, asking if two carpenters could be trained. "No carpenters are going to use my lathes," he drawled, "but I'll give priority to your carpenters for getting the sanding done on those braces."*

Sanding the braces continued to slow assembly. By the end of that hot summer month he learned from the other supervisors that Max had always been very possessive of the jobs within his department, fearing that other departments might take away some of his work. Max suffered from territorial control. He didn't see the big picture and only focused on his primary team, not the other teams to which he belonged. By the end of August, with production slowing, Josh asked his boss for help. Max had been having other difficulties and had requested a transfer. By Thanksgiving he was replaced by someone with a reputation for teamwork. Josh had learned a valuable lesson about territorial control and how it can reduce team effectiveness and bottom line profits.

TEAM ROLE IN DECISION MAKING

Your role as a team member will be different depending on the managing style of your team's decision maker. If all team members understand their roles, decisions will be made more quickly and implemented more effectively. What part are you expected to play in the decision-making process?

As a new team member you must first understand how your team makes decisions, then assume the proper role as soon as possible. The best place to start learning your team's decision-making process is to use the same stereotypes discussed in the chapter on boss's managing styles (authoritarian vs. concensus), chapter 7. Compare your team's process to these stereotypes. Once you've established where on the continuum — authoritarian vs. concensus — your team lies, then you can determine the role you will be expected to play.

Authoritarian Style

In this style the manager consults team members, then makes the decision as an individual. Team members have four responsibilities:

BEFORE DECISION
Before the decision give your manager your candid opinions and alternatives. Resist the temptation to present only one side (your preference) of the story. Present persuasive evidence to the best of your ability, knowing that the decision then rests with your manager.

WHEN DECISION IS MADE
When your manager makes his decision accept it. Don't waste time arguing, or behaving in any way that could be considered disloyal. After all, in an authoritarian model your responsibility for input ends before the decision is made. There is only one exception: see "problems with the decision."

IMPLEMENTING DECISION
After the decision has been made, support it and work to make that decision a success. Don't be tempted to voice disagreement to others.

PROBLEMS WITH DECISION
Communicate problems and changed — or changing — conditions to your manager so decisions can be modified, if necessary. When reporting problems, be prepared to offer constructive suggestions for improvement, if asked. It is not appropriate to suggest that another decision should have been made instead.

Consensus Style

The decision is made by agreement of all team members. Your responsibilities when on a consensus-style team are as follows:

BEFORE THE DECISION
Before the decision is made make sure all team members — not just your manager — understand your opinions and alternatives.

WHEN DECISION IS MADE
During the decision-making process contribute to the group's agreement. Don't spend time supporting unrealistic alternatives which you hold as an individual agenda. Listen carefully to the viewpoints of others. Reflect on everyone else's comments in light of future consequences with regard to your department, region and company.

IMPLEMENTING DECISION
After the decision has been made, take ownership of it. After all, it is your team's decision, a decision which inherently holds your input. Making it a success makes your team a success, which makes you a success.

PROBLEMS WITH DECISION
Make other team members and your manager aware of any problems and changed — or changing — conditions which may affect this team decision. When pointing out potential problems always include possible solutions.

What Graduates Should Know:

MORE IMPORTANT IN BUSINESS
  *Because of the intense competition in the private sector teamwork is more important in business than in other organizations.

MULTI-LEVEL TEAMS
  *Grads will be members of several different teams within the same company at the same time. How well grads understand the different goals of each team and are able to blend these goals will determine a great deal of the grad's successes.

TEAM DEPENDENCY
  *Every team is dependent on all team members completing their assigned functions on specified deadlines. Grads tend to overlook deadlines. Be aware of the importance of deadlines.

TERRITORIAL CONTROL
*Team members who over-control their territories
and won't accommodate larger team goals are
detrimental to the company's business success.

TEAM ROLE IN DECISION MAKING
*Learn your role in decision making by comparing
roles in the two managing styles with the unique
traits of your team.

———————

Chapter 12

COMMUNICATIONS

This chapter will save you frustration and embarrassment. This promise will be realized when you grasp and use two simple rules: the "Least Formal" rule and the "Cool Down" rule. In addition, it provides business communication etiquette and several effective tools to improve your ability to communicate in business.

VERBAL COMMUNICATIONS

In business the very words you speak will be the basis of the opinions others form about you. Those opinions, in turn, will form the basis of the recommendations others make for or against you achieving success in your career. As discussed in chapter 1, "Differences Between School and Business," most of your communication in school was written; in business 80% of your communication will be verbal.

Influencing Others

Your ability to influence and motivate others to understand your positions and beliefs is critical to your success. You'll be judged by what you say and how you say it, whether in the one-on-one discussions with your manager, peers and subordinates, or in your participation during meetings. Observe carefully the verbal skills successful managers in your organization have. Notice the way they present their ideas, the way they listen, the way they ask questions of others. Practice your verbal skills with others by imitating the successful methods others model for you.

Cindy was very proud of landing her first job out of college, an inspector for a large, well-known fast food chain. Travelling a three-state area, she tried to get to know her restaurant managers better than if she had to communicate only over the phone, by letter or by FAX. Cindy began feeling some of her managers were defensive and argumentative. She talked to her boss, Mark, about her concerns. Mark suggested he accompany her on her next round of visits to the store managers. After visiting just two stores, Mark made an observation. "You know your product, no doubt about that. But you're talking too much and not listening enough, Cindy. You're coming off as a know-it-all. All your managers are older — and not just older, but more experienced than you — and, I suspect, they don't think you're showing them enough respect. Try listening to what they're saying. Compliment them and ask them what they plan to do to correct the problems that they bring up. In other words, treat them like experienced, professional managers. If you think your way would be better, express it positively by starting out every criticism with : Have you considered trying . . . (then give them your positive idea) I think all you need to do is practice using a little respectful diplomacy."

Cindy had been talking a lot. She had wanted her store managers to see her as knowledgeable and professional. Maybe she had overdone it. She listened to Mark's advice. During the next several months she practiced listening attentively, showing respect and being positive. Her managers' attitudes seemed to improve dramatically. Within three months Mark said two of her managers had commented on how much her advice had helped and how they appreciated her showing concern for their businesses!

Most Important Skill

Remember your most important skill depends on your ability to communicate with others. You want to create positive relationships; that means communicating with them verbally. You will be required to find out what people really want by listening to what they say and how they say it. Cindy had listened carefully to her managers. When she heard them becoming defensive — and became aware of their arguments — she learned to step back, to ask questions in nonthreatening ways and to listen. Not only did she learn about her managers, but by listening to their ideas for improving productivity she learned what they really expected. Cindy was a quick-study of "how" things were said. She used all the tools she could to fully understand what the other meant — as well as what they said. With verbal communication you have the benefit of observing how others say what they say: the tones they use and the inflections in their voices. These actions will give you more clues on how important the topic of conversation is to them. You will want to communicate precisely to others what you need or want, leaving the least amount of room for misunderstanding. In the process, you'll want to use a great deal of tact and respect. Think about what you say and think about how it will affect others with whom you are talking or those who might be listening.

Telephone

The telephone can be one of your most useful tools. Learn to use its capabilities and complexities and it will reward you. It has more capacity than simply a one-on-one voice communication. Arrange conference calls, use your modem to receive voice mail and to send and receive FAXs. Some of the more experienced employees (those who have been around the longest) may choose not to learn these skills. If you are adept at using these modern and time-saving conveniences you will free up more time for yourself, which will allow you to accomplish more.

The telephone should never be used as a substitute for face-to-face meetings, but it is a valuable addition to the communication that is so vital to everyday business relationships, as Cindy learned quickly.

One of her managers called and requested a telephone update before the monthly computer reports were generated. His opinion of her and how they worked together was important to Cindy. She thought of how communicating these reports daily might help all her managers. She checked with Mark about her idea. He approved of sending all managers a daily, group voice mail update. It would only take five minutes each day with the new telephone system's group voice-mail capabilities. It might be very helpful to the managers; they'd try it for three months.

At the end of the trial period all of the managers felt that getting their numbers daily helped them reduce costs. Cindy was pleased she had found a way to easily communicate needed information that saved her managers money and at the same time strengthened their relationships with her. She was happy when several of her managers later told her boss how much the daily report continued to help.

WRITTEN COMMUNICATIONS

Say It Before You Write It

There are some simple rules in written communications. Whenever you write anything, you create a record that may come back to haunt you in the future. Keeping this in mind, the best solution is to say it rather than to write it. Be very careful what you write — be sure it is necessary and well thought out.

Unless you're in the legal department, writing will probably be a small part of what you do. Typically, little of your communication will be written; the majority will be spoken. Always take an extra amount of care when communicating in writing.

Clarity and Brevity

Be clear and brief in what you communicate, but especially in what you write. In business it's the short papers with concise, clear paragraphs and outline format that work best. Use lots of headings and an executive summary.

There's a big difference between what is expected and rewarded in school and what is expected and rewarded in business. One graduate described it best by saying, "In school you take a three-page idea and turn it into a six-page paper. In business you take a three-page idea and reduce it to a one-page outline starting with a summary paragraph."

Business people want to use their time most efficiently. That means taking the least amount of time to read. Changing your writing style from long, complex sentences and paragraphs (common in school) to short, concise paragraphs (common in business) will require more writing time. Condensing and clearly stating an idea takes much more time to write and much less time to read. I recall a story told to me once about Ben Franklin who, it was said, wrote at the end of a rather long letter an apology, saying he didn't have time to express his thoughts in a short letter.

Company Format

Company formatting is important. Each company has its own way of formatting correspondence: FAXS, memos, letters and reports. Learn how to format using the tools your company provides. Learn what those within your company expect and do it the way they want it done.

The "Least Formal" Rule

As a general rule you'll want to use the least formal means of communication that will adequately communicate what you need to get across. This applies to both written and verbal communication. A one-on-one discussion is preferable to a meeting. A phone call, or a talk in the office, would be preferable to a letter or memo. It takes less time and makes the communication "less official." If it's something that must be written, a note is better than a memo, a memo is better than a letter, a letter is better than a report. The less formal rule is good because it saves time, puts less in a permanent form and requires fewer levels of approval before action can be taken.

The "Cool Down" Rule

In business, if you write anything when you are angry or frustrated — anything that could be misunderstood or get you into trouble — you should have a rule that it be held overnight and reviewed the next day before it's sent. Many managers have an understanding with their secretaries that negative correspondence automatically gets put in the desk overnight. Take a look at it in the light of a new day and a rested frame of mind. Remember that those successful in business can rarely afford the luxury of expressing anger. If the letter is still necessary, reword it before sending it. It may feel good to get things off your chest, but it doesn't enhance your positive relationships with others to mail it. Rethink, reword, and keep it positive.

Computer

Anything entered into computers — e-mail, documents, files or calendars — should be considered to have the same permanence and possible wide distribution as written communication. Therefore, all the rules that apply to written communication apply to anything entered in your computer.

Be especially aware that the convenience of e-mail and the ease with which it is sent, tempts us to communicate without thoroughly thinking through a situation: namely our anger or criticism. These are normally best expressed face-to-face. If this is not possible, develop a personal procedure to delay computer entries which would be considered critical at least until the following day. This gives you time to reconsider your point of view, the other person's point of view and what is best for your company and all involved.

Computers offer excellent opportunities for grads to demonstrate technical skills and knowledge. Wise use of a computer's communication capabilities will give you an advantage over older, slower-to-change employees.

What Grads Should Know:

VERBAL
>   *Influencing Others - Your ability to influence and motivate others with your words is critical to achieving a successful career in business

>   *Most Important Skill - Your ability to establish positive relationships depends on your verbal communication skills

*Telephone - Make sure you never substitute the telephone for personal, face-to-face contact. Learn to use all the capabilities of your phone system.

WRITTEN
*Clarity and Brevity - Take the time to acquire the skill of writing short and concise communications.

*"Least Formal" Rule - Select the least formal method that is appropriate: verbal before written, memo before letter, note before memo, etc.

*"Cool Down" Rule - Hold overnight any words written in anger; be smart and don't send it.

COMPUTER
*The same written communication rules apply to anything entered into the computer.

Chapter 13

MAKING MISTAKES POSITIVE

Quick Reference

- "It's Not My Fault" Response
- Choosing a Response
- Producers Make Mistakes
- Mistakes as Opportunities
- Your Plan To Show Excellence
- What Grads Should Know

A mistake provides an excellent opportunity to show how good you are. This chapter gives you the six steps to create your own plan to correct mistakes. You'll now be able to turn a negative into a positive and look better than if you'd never made any mistake at all. Having this plan and implementing it will give you the confidence to produce more work and to be more successful in your first job.

"IT'S NOT MY FAULT" RESPONSE

Avoiding Responsibility Unsuccessfully

A popular — yet highly unsuccessful — response to mistakes is the "it's not my fault" response. We all have used it as children and have modified it somewhat as adults. We like to think we don't use it. Unfortunately it takes many disguises, all damaging to a greater or lesser extent.

Unsuccessful Techniques

Techniques we use in this response vary, but usually include a variety of defenses.

AVOID THINKING ABOUT IT: Deny it and maybe it will go away, maybe it really didn't happen.

COVER IT UP: Nobody will find out; there will be no penalty if it's never found.

IGNORE IT: So they found out . . . maybe they'll forget about it or get tired of hearing about it and will drop it.

PLEAD IGNORANCE: Was that a mistake? I didn't know it was wrong.

DENY IT: I didn't do it; it wasn't me.

MAKE EXCUSES: I didn't have the right information; the data was misleading.

BLAME OTHERS: They did it; I couldn't have, I was on vacation.

BE A MARTYR: "I take full responsibility" (which everyone knows really means that I didn't do it, but I'm such a good person I'll take the blame).

CHOOSING A RESPONSE

The "it's not my fault" response, in any of its forms, is not productive for someone who wants to succeed in business. It creates a bad impression within management. Mistakes are highly visible situations to your boss and other managers. This response makes you look as if you lack character, confidence, ethics and integrity. It makes you look weak, lacking in management potential.

"It's not my fault" draws more attention to your mistake, making it take longer to correct because everyone involved wastes valuable energy making excuses and blaming others. The actions you take with the "it's not my fault" response are usually much worse than your original mistake. You can choose to use this situation as an opportunity, however. First, you should realize: producers make mistakes.

PRODUCERS MAKE MISTAKES

An alternative response to making mistakes is to avoid them altogether. You might cautiously reduce the volume and the risk of your actions. You could become so cautious that you double- and triple-check everything before you do it. You might reduce the amount you do, avoiding mistakes by avoiding the situations containing potential errors. You could do only the safe things that you are absolutely sure wouldn't cause mistakes.

Being cautious to a fault is like the water skier who was proud he'd been water skiing for ten years without falling. He hadn't fallen because he'd never taken risks; he hadn't done anything but stay directly behind the boat and avoid falling.

Inactivity and extreme caution will produce poor performance and minimal results. In order to achieve maximum results you must produce a high volume of quality work and take well-thought-out, calculated risks. Producers make mistakes. They are human; despite careful planning and striving to do the best job, mistakes are bound to happen.

It is important that you make every effort to avoid mistakes, but once made use them as an opportunity to show how good you are.

MISTAKES AS OPPORTUNITIES

Mistakes are unusually high visibility situations that, unfortunately, draw more attention than almost any other important situation. They are of more concern to your manager — and other managers — because your mistakes become their mistakes. It is your boss who is responsible for your actions and who takes some of the blame for your mistakes.

If you recover from a mistake — showing how good your work can be and how committed you are — you may be able to surprise and impress those above you. They expect the "it's not my fault response" or, minimally, caution and inactivity on your part. The contrast of someone who makes an excellent recovery with a maximum effort will be more significant and memorable to them than if you had done a good job in the first place.

A mistake is an important opportunity to show how good you are. What you need is a plan to correct mistakes and turn them into a demonstration of excellence.

YOUR PLAN TO SHOW EXCELLENCE

The Six-Step Plan

To take full advantage of changing that mistake into an opportunity you should have the six-step plan for excellence. Your six-step plan to respond to mistakes includes each of the following:
1) establish preventive procedures
2) analyze the mistake and prepare a solution
3) admit it and recommend a solution
4) maximize your effort
5) change preventive procedures
6) communicate to management

1) Establish Preventive Procedures

Reasonable procedures should be established to prevent mistakes in the beginning. Levels of authority, checks and verification — whatever is necessary to eliminate potential mistakes — should be set in place. All mistakes will be evaluated to see if reasonable standards were in place to prevent mistakes. Look at your job and evaluate vulnerable areas. Set up procedures to catch mistakes before they happen. Take the example of Tony, who had built up a number of checks and verifications after his predecessor had been let go just two years earlier.

Tony was a very organized, successful sales representative with 11 beverage store customers. Every three months his company produced new advertising and price displays. Tony always checked the prices with corporate sales to ensure they were based on the correct volume. He also made sure Ann, the distribution clerk, never sent out displays without his OK; this was his check to prevent any errors. So far, so good ... but mistakes can happen even with the best laid plans.

2) Analyze Mistakes; Prepare Solutions

Don't rush to communicate mistakes. Identify them, analyze them and prepare an alternative solution or solutions. It is very important to have accurate facts about the extent of the mistake and what harm it caused. A rush to communicate can create more mistakes and mislead management.

Tony knew the July 1 price changes would normally go out during his vacation, but he knew Ann would hold them until he got back so he could check them before they were sent to his accounts. When Tony returned he found that Ann had been sick and his prices had gone out with four errors. Tony knew he was in big trouble; these four errors went to his four largest volume customers. Tony spent all of his first morning back finding out what prices had been communicated, how it had happened, the extent of the damage, and how he might correct the problem.

3) Admit It and Recommend a Solution

Admit your mistake in a positive way, starting out with your intended solution. Recommend the best solution with any other possible solutions. Give the reasons you selected what you think is the best one. When you admit the mistake, do it frankly without blaming others or making excuses. Be sure to acknowledge the severity of any damage the mistake has or will cause. Make sure you also acknowledge your own disappointment, that this mistake is not up to your personal high standards of performance. By doing this, others will realize you understand what has happened and that you are adequately concerned. Do not gloss over the mistake nor the consequences.

Use the words: "I made the mistake." If someone working with you made it say "We made the mistake." Don't hint that it may not be yours by saying, "I take responsibility. . . ."

After researching what had happened, how and to what extent, Tony went to his boss, Andy, and said he would like permission to visit his 4 customers in the next two days. He told Andy of his plan to personally deliver revised displays, that he had made a mistake by being on vacation when the prices went out. Andy was justifiably mad, "You knew when the prices were going out, yet you scheduled vacation anyway?"

Tony made no excuses. He explained about the check and verification system and also how unfortunate it was that Ann had been sick the very day the price changes were to go out. Andy cooled down considerably when he realized Tony had set up a procedure to avoid the incident, but that a series of unfortunate situations had come together to create the error. Tony took a deep breath, "It's my mistake. I should have called Ann the day the prices were to go out to double-check. I know how important price changes are and I'm going to do everything I can to correct this with our accounts immediately." Tony knew he would have to maximize his efforts to show he both realized the damage and was concerned that it be remedied.

4) Maximize Effort

Make an all-out effort to correct mistakes. This is where you impress management on how good you are. Don't spare any time, effort or resources to make the best possible correction in the shortest time. Make a big deal out of it. The extra time and effort shows your concern and your personal commitment to excellence.

Come early. Stay late. Image is important here, so even if it's not necessary do it anyway. It shows your positive attitude and how much correcting mistakes means to you.

Before leaving Andy's office, Tony explained that he had already corrected the prices and they would be printed in the morning. Before and during lunch he had called all four customers and alerted them to the mistake. He asked Andy if he could visit two customers on Friday and two on Saturday. He would help them make necessary changes, set up their displays and make sure they were well prepared for the start of the sale Monday morning. Andy agreed, "It's a good idea to personally go out and help them. It'll impress them that we're really concerned about their sales."

As Tony was walking out of Andy's office, thanking him for his support, Andy said "I appreciate you spending your Saturday to get this thing corrected." Andy's recognition that Tony was giving maximum effort was exactly what he wanted. Andy realized how much correcting this mistake meant to Tony.

5) Change Preventive Procedures

Change procedures to prevent this or any related mistake from happening in the future. This is important because it shows management you are an organized, careful person who cares about preventing mistakes. Make sure you use the same maximum effort to set up preventive procedures and complete these in the shortest possible time. Make all corrections visible. Be sure everyone involved in the mistake understands the preventive procedure. Make sure you do more than your share in preparing these procedures. Lastly, be positive toward everyone involved.

All four of Tony's accounts were pleased with his additional efforts and by Sunday Tony was feeling redeemed. Now he'd just have to insure there would never be a repeat performance of this error. On Monday morning Tony worked with Ann to prepare a written procedure to distribute prices. He made sure it included a warning not to send any price information to customers until he — or the acting customer service representative — had approved it.

Ann thanked Tony for not blaming her. Tony gained innumerable points with Ann when he said, "It was my mistake; I knew the prices were changing; I should have called."

6) Communicate to Management

Communicate the corrections you made both verbally and in writing and include a copy of the procedure(s) you set up to prevent it from happening again. As with all written procedures, have your manager (and any others involved) approve it before sending. This is an important step in showing management that the mistake has been corrected and tells them how much effort you made in correcting it.

Tony met with his boss Monday afternoon and told him about the approval he'd received from his accounts, "Two of my customers told me that with all the price errors they'd witnessed over the years, this was the first time any supplier had helped them make the corrections and set up their displays." Andy was pleased, "Good job, your efforts show you care about doing a good job."

Tony went one step further. He prepared a memo that afternoon explaining the mistake and what he had done to correct it. He attached a copy of the procedure he and Ann had prepared and gave it to Andy. Impressed, Andy passed out copies of the memo at the next staff meeting and told all the service reps what a good job Tony had done.

Mistakes will happen to any successful grad, manager, or even to senior managers. When they are unavoidable, your job is to know how to recover from each mistake more favorably than when you went into it.

What Grads Should Know:

"IT'S NOT MY FAULT" RESPONSE
  *Using "it's not my fault" as a response to a mistake only makes a negative situation worse.

PRODUCERS MAKE MISTAKES
  *Keep your production high and don't be afraid to take calculated risks.

 MISTAKES: OPPORTUNITIES TO SHOW HOW GOOD YOU ARE!
  *If you have a good plan to correct mistakes you can turn a negative into a positive.

YOUR PLAN TO SHOW EXCELLENCE
  *The Six Steps to Correct Mistakes:
    -1) Establish Preventive Procedures
    -2) Analyze Mistakes, Prepare Solutions
    -3) Admit and Recommend a Solution
    -4) Maximize Effort to Correct Mistake
    -5) Change Preventive Procedures
    -6) Communicate to Management

Chapter 14

IDEAL BUSINESS IMAGE

Quick Reference

- Components of Business Image
- Best Place to Start
- Selecting Your Professional Image
- Dress Rules and Guidelines
- Appropriate is Best
- Fashion Competency
- The "Uniform" Mentality: Mix and Match
- What Grads Should Know

A costly mistake is believing a "professional and conservative business image" is just a lot of hoopla. Remember it is the older managers who determine who will meet their expectations and they are the decision makers on promotions. This chapter tells you what managers expect and how to achieve a professional business image with the least effort and expense.

COMPONENTS OF BUSINESS IMAGE

There are three main components of business image: wardrobe, accessories and grooming. Which is most important? Which will get you that promotion? Understanding the principles of business image and their importance in your success will make your job of attaining it that much easier.

Wardrobe

Your wardrobe, the clothing you wear, speaks loudly about the type of person you are. This is especially true for managers who observe you but don't work with you. You want to send the message, "I'm senior management potential." You can speak loudly to them about your desire to succeed through dressing professionally, yet conservatively. Appropriate attire is essential and the best business appearance is the one that is not only professional, but proper and fitting for your company, your location and your responsibilities.

Accessories

Accessories can reinforce your professionalism. Take care in the type of briefcase, ties, scarves, shoes and jewelry you choose. Make them attest to the conservative and professional approach with which you view your career.

Grooming

Your grooming might not land you that promotion, but not being well groomed surely would sabotage your chances for consideration. Carefully groom yourself and continually evaluate your clothing for cleanliness, neatness and appropriateness.

BEST PLACE TO START

A well groomed and professional physical image is a basic requirement to be successful in business. You must look the part of the well-groomed professional before you can be eligible for promotion. A grad's image should be a high priority because she is perceived as being young and inexperienced. If you have a good business appearance you'll fit the image of an older, more experienced employee and will appear more mature and ready for promotion. It is, therefore, even more important that you make an effort to not only act professional but also to look professional.

Underestimating the importance of image — because it seems superficial — may be a costly mistake. In reality, image may be the only way you are judged at all in the first several months — or years — by most managers. Many will probably have no other contact with you than observing your appearance. This is one of the quickest and easiest adjustments you can make now.

If you know in advance where you'll be working, concentrate on your business image several weeks before you start. Your goal is to look "just right" every day, a goal overlooked by Dan in his efforts to be first in sales.

Dan walked into the first floor of his company's unassuming building his first day on the job. He wore slacks and a sport coat; everybody else dressed in dark suits. "At least I wore a sport coat," he chuckled a year later over a beer with several of his co-workers, "I'd never do that again. I was clueless about how to dress or about what was expected of me. The only suit I owned was one I wore to an occasional wedding or to my grandfather's funeral." Dan should have observed the dress practices during the interview process.

If your recruiter or interviewer hasn't told you, call the human resources department and ask what dress standard is expected by your company. At the very least, find out before your first day on the job.

Imagining Success

"Imagining success" is a valuable exercise to help you see yourself as others see you. Walk through a crowd of people and imagine how successful each person is currently. Imagine yourself as a senior manager with 25 years of success. Imagine that you've been through a lot with your company, that it's part of you now. Then imagine that you eye a newly-hired graduate and ride the elevator together. You notice how she's dressed, how she's groomed and ask yourself: *How is she representing this company? Is she neat, organized, professional? Does she have the right image?* You make an unconscious note about how successful you believe she'll be. . . .

Now, after imagining that you were a successful manager looking at a new grad, how successful do you think you look to others who are observing you? Do you look the part of a potential senior manager to an accomplished manager within your new company?

A Costly Mistake

Consider Brendan, whose first job suited his interest in hockey: selling hockey equipment to sporting goods stores. Being a casual guy, he felt comfortable enough to "dress down," telling his friends it was his unique style, even though others wore suits. Proving himself a hotshot in sales, his territory was third best in the country and his sales were the highest of any first-year grad. When the large accounts sales rep was promoted, Brendan knew he'd be considered for the job. He was successful and ambitious, if not just a little bit cocky. Being single now worked in his favor; he could travel extensively, which was a real plus.

He told his manager, Beth, he wanted the job, then he applied and waited. Two months later his company announced the position had been filled from outside.

"From outside!" Brendan felt confused, angry and frustrated. Beth agreed to talk with him that evening after researching how the decision had been made. Beth had always liked Brendan and recognized his potential. In her office she gave Brendan the difficult news. "Management is impressed with your sales ability, Brendan. You've had much early success within the company. You're one of my best and I want to see you go far. I'm going to be candid. What I heard is that you don't 'look ready for promotion.' They wanted to hire from the inside. However, the large accounts rep must call on purchasing departments, typically more formal than our retail stores. They felt whoever represented us needed more experience and polish. It's our business image, you know."

No, Brendan didn't know. He felt hurt. His sales suffered the following two months before it dawned on him: this was just one more area he had to learn about — learn what was expected — learn how to adjust — learn how to look professional. He was honest with himself, honest enough to realize he didn't have the experience to know what was the best professional image for his company. He needed help. He needed the right image.

SELECTING YOUR PROFESSIONAL IMAGE

Brendan knew it was important to select an image that could advance his career. He needed to find an image that was successful and proven to be promotable.

Brendan looked for several people who were recognized and who had been promoted within the company. He did not choose another graduate, even though he thought a couple of them dressed professionally. Neither did he limit himself to just one level up, his manager's level, but jumped a level to that of his boss's boss.

Brendan chose three fast-track managers whose promotions proved they had the right appearance. They were all conservatively-dressed middle managers two levels above him. Brendan closely observed their wardrobe, accessories and grooming. He mentally formed a composite image and set about duplicating it, with the help of a salesman at a reputable clothing store. When promoted two years later he was convinced the image changes he had made were a big part of management's decision to promote him.

DRESS RULES AND GUIDELINES

Rules

To help you identify a professional image, here are a few straight-forward dress rules and guidelines. Modify these rules by the guidelines in this section and you'll impress those managers who observe you.

FORMAL AND CONSERVATIVE
Generally, when in doubt or when given a choice, tend toward formal rather than informal, conservative rather than fashionable, dress up not down, and always on the side of being professional.

Specifically lean toward being formal and conservative. Age dictates dress habits in many managers, but a contemporary equivalent is always available. If your company has casual days on Friday or during the summer, always tend toward the most formal, conservative side of casual. When in doubt, visit a clothing store with a reputation for prestigious labels. Look — even if you don't yet buy.

Guidelines

GUIDELINES FOR MALES
In your business do most younger men wear sport coats and slacks while senior male managers wear suits? You should start wearing suits.

In your office do some male managers wear informal, colored suits (brown, tan and light colors) while senior managers wear dark blues and charcoals? You should wear dark blues and charcoals.

In your company do only some managers wear ties with no one wearing jackets? Always wear a tie.

GUIDELINES FOR FEMALES
In your organization do some female managers wear dresses and some wear suits? You should wear suits.

In your company do some female managers wear brightly colored suits and some wear formal, darker colors? You should wear darker colored suits.

In manufacturing plants do some female managers wear jeans and some wear slacks? You should wear slacks.

Remember: if you error, do so in favor of the formal, dressing up not down, always striving to look professional.

APPROPRIATE IS BEST

Again, the best business image is one that is professional and fitting for your company, location and responsibilities. One of your main goals is to fit in, not to be different. What is appropriate in New York may not be appropriate in L.A., even within the same department of the same company. There are even differences between departments within an organization. What is "best" is most appropriate for your situation.

When you visit your company — in the location you'll be working — be very observant of what is worn and by whom. Large cities tend to be more formal than smaller towns. Downtowns tend to be more formal than the suburbs. The East Coast tends to be more formal than the West Coast. Within organizations the sales departments tend to be more formal than the production departments. Finance tends to be more formal than sales.

You may or may not feel competent when it comes to fashion and style. If not, it's no problem. You simply solve this dilemma as any other: seek sources of expertise to get the information and help you need. Find a fashion advisor if you don't have the interest, nor the energy, for putting it together yourself.

FASHION COMPETENCY

If you've worked in a clothing store you may know the kinds of materials which hold up, which will prove to be a valuable investment in your future and which won't. What is your level of fashion competency? Do you know a dark wool suit from a light polyester? If you have achieved a level of fashion know-how it's another skill which will be very helpful to you. If you're more like Brendan and have only rarely donned a suit, don't despair. Help can be found from two very reliable sources: your local clothing retailer of good reputation, or from several excellent books.

First, find a local retailer with an excellent reputation for stocking quality attire for those within your business community. A good suit will be a valuable investment in your future and, like most good investments, will not be cheap. Second, locate a salesperson to assist you who looks professional and conservative. Be honest about your level of competence in shopping for clothing, what clothes you currently have and what you think you'll need. Let them know what you're prepared to spend. Then adjust to your "learning mode." You may learn a number of valuable ideas about current fashion trends. Or, you may learn that you have no interest in fashion and that your best bet is to lean on a professional as your personal fashion consultant, accessory coordinator and purchasing agent. By helping you succeed in attaining a professional business appearance, you will return and perhaps send referrals to them.

Now you understand the importance of maintaining a professional business image. You know the components which include wardrobe, accessories and grooming. You recognize the dress rules and guidelines and can factor in the appropriateness of formality to your particular business.

The last, most important criteria to dressing successfully will be your own attitude of consistency. Consistency guarantees you'll project your best professional image all the time with the greatest ease, the least effort and for the best value. The easiest way to accomplish this is to develop a "uniform" mentality.

THE "UNIFORM" MENTALITY:
MIX AND MATCH

You never know when an unexpected opportunity will arise where your image will impress management. For this reason you'll always want to look your professional, conservative best. Consider your business attire nothing more than a uniform. Your goal: project that best business image every day.

What is the easiest way to achieve this? Use the mix and match, or "uniform" mentality. Many successful business people consciously choose their entire wardrobe to mix and match. Every suit can be worn with every shirt or blouse, tie or scarf, adding belts, shoes and accessories for variety. A modification of this would be to choose two or three suits which have their own two or three variations of ties or scarves, shirts or blouses, shoes and interchangeable accessories.

Returning to Brendan's story, Brendan realized he'd have to consider his business attire not as an extension of who he was, but as an extension of the job he wanted. With the help of a professional-looking sales clerk Brendan purchased three suits: one blue, one navy and another charcoal. He bought black shoes, socks and burgundy ties. Along with that he bought ten long-sleeved white shirts. Every shirt coordinated with every tie and every tie went great with every suit. Brendan learned to like it. He dropped off one suit and five shirts at the laundry weekly so his wardrobe was low maintenance and professionally conservative.

That's great for men. But women like more individuality in their attire, you say. As a professional you may find as much individuality as you need if you have even three to five quality, conservative, professional suits with alternate accessories. A tremendous variety of blouses, scarves, jewelry and accessory pieces are still available. Save on big expense items (like suits) and treat yourself to a gift of something else. Your conservative and professional "uniform" mentality will get you further — faster — than demanding individuality and attention through creative dressing.

This uniform mentality is an easy answer to those who don't want to spend energy shopping for, coordinating and maintaining a unique — and soon-to-be-outdated — wardrobe.

Uniform mentality is not only a time-saver and headache-saver, it is also a money-saver. You'll avoid the early morning frustration and waste of time deciding what to wear. You'll save the embarrassment of feeling thrown together if you ensure your "uniforms" are cleaned and hung in order for the week. You'll save money by mixing and matching, instead of having a separate outfit for each day.

Most importantly, you'll have achieved your goal of the consistent, conservative and professional business appearance.

What Grads Should Know:

COMPONENTS OF BUSINESS IMAGE
   *Your business image is made up of wardrobe,
      accessories and grooming.

BEST PLACE TO START
   *Grads are perceived to be young and inexperienced.
      The easiest and quickest adjustment you can make to
      look more mature and promotable is to acquire a
      professional, conservative image.

SELECTING YOUR PROFESSIONAL IMAGE
*Choose several professional-looking managers two
levels above you who have been promoted within the
company. Observe their wardrobes, accessories and
grooming to form your personal image to imitate.

DRESS RULES AND GUIDELINES
*Always dress more formally and conservatively rather
than less formally and casually.

APPROPRIATE IS BEST
*The best business image is the one that is appropriate to
your unique working situation. Be aware of
differences within your company.

"UNIFORM" MENTALITY: MIX AND MATCH
*Plan your wardrobe and accessories so all parts match
and all provide you with a formal, conservative look.
*You never know when an opportunity will appear to
impress management. Have the same professional
look every day.

Chapter 15

PERSONAL LIFE

Quick Reference

- Importance to Your Career
- Be Concerned with Your Image
- Keep Your Private Life Private
- Finances, Relationships and Time
  - Financial Responsibility
  - Personal Relationships
  - Personal Time
- Your Company's "Acceptable Standards"
- What Grads Should Know

Your personal life can be very important to your career. Most companies unofficially require you to meet minimum standards before you're promoted beyond a certain level. If you know those standards in advance you can make sure you fit the image that will get you promoted. What if you choose to pay no attention to the standards your company sets? Then don't read this chapter.

IMPORTANCE TO YOUR CAREER

In order to be eligible for promotion past a certain level, most companies will unofficially evaluate your personal life to make sure it meets their minimum standards. The level and the standards vary from company to company, but almost all companies have some concern about your personal life.

Employees represent their company and are part of its overall image to customers, investors and the public. The higher up employees are in the company the more their personal lives will reflect the image that company has within the community. Top managers who are out of control in their personal lives are suspected by outside investors and customers of making mistakes in running their companies.

BE CONCERNED WITH YOUR IMAGE

If you desire a successful career you should be concerned with the image your personal life presents. Even though it may not be too significant in your first job or two, eventually it becomes an issue; it's always easier to start out with an acceptable image rather than have to change it later.

Company standards traditionally are set by the forty-year-old senior manager. Grads can have difficulty conforming to this more conservative standard because of age and generational differences. As grads grow older they become more conservative. At the same time their company standards become more modernized to fit them. A blending takes place as conservative and progressive merge.

KEEP YOUR PRIVATE LIFE PRIVATE

As a general rule the safest decision for a grad to make is to keep your private life private. Choose friends and activities outside your company and keep them separate. This is safe for two reasons: 1) It gives you the first few years to assess your company's "acceptable standards" for your personal life, and 2) It gives you some private time to relax, to be yourself and to adjust to your more formal, conservative role at work. It allows you time to make the adjustments from a student to a business person without always being "on stage."

The exception to this is when you're sure your activities or interests will benefit your image at work. Examples of sure winners that will enhance your work image are golf or membership in community or industry business clubs or organizations. This list of "sure winners" is very short and is limited to your company's products or business objectives.

FINANCES, RELATIONSHIPS
AND TIME

Business may have some concerns with these three major components — and most personal aspects — of a grad's personal life, including:

1) financial responsibility
2) personal relationships
3) personal time

The possible business image concerns are listed at the end of the section.

Financial Responsibility

Showing financial responsibility will be an indicator to your managers about your ability to make good financial decisions.

The most common financial mistake grads make is to incur a large amount of debt by not controlling their spending. When you add credit card debt for needed business clothes and apartment basics to school loans, many grads end up with a high percentage of their income paying off debt. What is affordable to you can often be best understood as a percentage of take-home pay. These are guidelines, but you may find them invaluable your first year or two as you begin your life of financial responsibility. First, determine your take-home pay in advance by subtracting taxes and other deductions. To give you an idea of the percentage of your income that should go to debt and other living expenses, compare your expenses to these averages:

EXPENSE	% OF INCOME
Housing (rent, insurance, utilities)	25%
Food (all meals at home or out)	10%
Transportation (mass transit and auto expense)	10%
Clothing (accessories and grooming)	10%
Spending (entertainment, subscriptions, gifts,misc.)	10%
Savings	15%
Insurance (life, casualty, all expenses: medical/dental)	5%
Debt	5%
Vacations and holidays	5%
Emergencies	5%
	100%

Try to arrange your expenses so they don't exceed these percentages. Remember, there are two ways to stay financially sound: increase income or decrease expenses. The first few years in your new job you may have more control over monitoring and controlling spending than in increasing your income.

Personal Relationships

Your personal relationships should be divided into two categories: 1) your private relationships with friends, family and acquaintances, and 2) your business social relationships, which include those people you accompany — or invite — as you attend social business occasions. These are further explained in "High Visibility Situations" (chapter 10).

PRIVATE RELATIONSHIPS

Concern about your private relationships is limited to those which 1) create problems with your job performance, 2) cause difficulty in the work place, or 3) are noticed negatively by other employees, customers or investors. Some managers believe that the selection of people you choose for private relationships indicates your ability to evaluate people in business. Evaluating people — as in selecting the best person for a job — is a skill which will be an important part of your future management skills.

These private relationships are those you have with spouse, children, other family members, friends, dates, acquaintances or members of organizations to which you belong. Because of the high level of legal, moral and ethical standards to which companies adhere, you should be aware of possible negative actions or effects caused by friends you make or organizations you join. Ask yourself: "Will this ever negatively affect my image within this company or any other company I may work for?"

As an example, you should be concerned about friends or groups that promote violence, discrimination, terrorism or any of the politically incorrect problems of which we are aware today. The most common mistake grads make in this area is in not realizing their company's moral or ethical standards may well be significantly more conservative than what was accepted in college. Associating with people who abused alcohol or illegal substances or who attended illegal demonstrations was overlooked or excused in school. These associations were justified; students were allowed to let off steam, or allowed their "youthful idealism." In the world of business overall judgement is evaluated and compared to other grads. If there is concern on any level that a grad's personal relationships may cause an image problem for the company, someone else will get the promotion that might have been awarded you.

BUSINESS SOCIAL RELATIONSHIPS
Review the points discussed in the chapter titled "High Visibility Situations" (chapter 10) before you decide whom to invite to any business social situation. If you aren't married choose that person carefully, taking into account the impression he will make. Consider his knowledge of business and social skills.

Whomever you choose to accompany you, whether spouse or friend, discuss the points covered in chapter 10, prior to the occasion. Give names and positions of key people. Explain any sensitive subjects to avoid. In short, prepare him so he will feel comfortable and will be able to help you make a good impression.

The ability to evaluate and select the right person for a job is an important skill in business. There is a tendency for some managers to evaluate a grad's ability to evaluate people by the people he selects for business social relationships. Be aware that these relationships may affect your business image positively if your choices are good — or negatively if your choices cause problems.

Personal Time

This refers to your time away from work spent on entertainment, hobbies, or recreation. It's important to recognize which activities can help your career, which can hurt your career and the stereotypes created about these activities by managers with whom you'll be working.

SWINGING SINGLES STEREOTYPE
Since most managers are older and married — and most grads are younger and single — there is a common stereotype among managers that grads are single swingers who have wild parties, take risks, abuse substances and generally live a wilder, more exciting lifestyle. Managers maintain that as grads grow older, become more mature and get married, they will then be ready for more responsibility and higher paying management jobs. If you are aware of this stereotype being perpetuated in your workplace you can counteract it by creating a more conservative, controlled — yes, even boring — image. This will go a long way in making you appear more mature, ready for increased responsibility and faster promotions. A major part of your mature, conservative image is choosing personal time activities that more closely parallel the interests of a forty-year-old manager.

If you prefer bar-hopping and bungi-jumping to golf and time with the kids, don't talk about it with the older employees at work. Again, the idea is to fit in and to perpetuate the solidarity of the company image, not to become the independent renegade, the risk-taker.

There's a big mistake many new grads make at their new company. A few of these forty-year-old managers will encourage grads to discuss their escapades and exploits. It is a mistake to do so regardless of whether they are bored with their own lives or have an honest interest in you. They might even be very interested in the more exciting swinging singles life you lead. They will encourage you to tell them about the more exciting things you do in your personal time. The mistake is in thinking this interest signals acceptance or approval. It does not. The best reaction is not to relate any of your personal time activities. Even one conversation can turn into office gossip; you could well be on your way of fitting the swinging singles stereotype, the very image you hope to avoid.

ACTIVITIES THAT CAN HELP YOUR CAREER

There are a few personal-time activities that may help your career. A good example of this is golf, the sport of business. If you are interested in sales, marketing or a senior management position, you should consider learning to play golf. It is a difficult, and often frustrating activity, but the number of successful forty-year-old managers who enjoy the game outnumber those in any other personal-time sport.

The only activity better than golf would be that which is most popular with the successful managers at your company. It would be time well spent to seek out the one activity that is most popular with the management of your company. If you develop an interest in this activity and are prepared to devote the time and energy to become a serious participant, it may reward you in the acquaintances you make and the friendships you form. That was Steve's experience as he looked back over his 15 successful years with the same company.

It was his first job out of the University of Colorado. His manufacturing company had a great reputation. He loved the

*location of their headquarters in Michigan overlooking Lake
Huron.*

*It was May when he'd arrived and he noticed that many of
the senior managers competed in weekly sail boat races during
the spring and summer. He'd never had an opportunity to sail,
or for that matter to live near a large body of water. But he
thought it sounded interesting and checked out some books on
sailing at the local library. He asked a friend who owned a
small sailboat to teach him what he could and even spent his
vacations in week-long sailing schools, or as a crew member
in weekend races.*

*Within four years he bought an M-20 sailboat, a popular
model with the senior managers. He joined the local race club
and began developing friendships with all the managers who
sailed. He continued to work diligently at his job, but began to
thoroughly enjoy his leisure time sailing and making friends
among those with similar interests.*

*After only 15 years he was promoted to Vice President of
Marketing, the youngest the company had ever experienced.
Steve was convinced that his friendships made during sailing
had helped him become successful earlier in his career than
would have been possible with only his hard work and diligence
to support him.*

YOUR COMPANY'S
"ACCEPTABLE STANDARDS"

The general standards of your personal life are not nearly as
important as the individual standards of your company. Your
success will depend on your knowing and adjusting to these
standards. To identify these use the same successful middle-

manager role models as discussed in "Good Work Habits," "New Skills" and "Ideal Business Image" (chapters 3, 4 and 14 respectively). As you learn how these managers meet your company's acceptable minimum standards you will have a basis to judge your own personal life.

Use the guidelines in this chapter which relate to your finances, your relationships and your time to evaluate the personal lives of your middle managers. Take your time. You won't have enough contact to make judgements initially, but keep watching for clues. In the meantime, keep your personal life separate. Look, listen and observe.

What Grads Should Know:

IMPORTANCE TO YOUR CAREER
  *Most companies will make an unofficial evaluation of
   your personal life before you can be promoted past a
   certain level.

KEEP YOUR PRIVATE LIFE PRIVATE
  *During your first few years keep your private life
   separate until you can assess your company's
   standards.

FINANCIAL RESPONSIBILITY
  *Control your spending within the recommended living
   expense percentages; reduce debt and save for the
   future.

PERSONAL RELATIONSHIPS AND TIME
  *Be aware of the average forty-year-old married
   manager's personal standards and be prepared to
   match them; avoid the swinging singles stereotype.

YOUR COMPANY'S "ACCEPTABLE STANDARDS"
*Every company is different. Use your middle manager's evaluations to assess your company's expectations.

Chapter 16

PREPARATION FOR FIRST DAY

An hour's research at this point gives you a week's advantage in understanding the big picture about your new company. Understanding the broader goals of your company helps you assimilate what is being said by those who have been around. When you know what to expect and how to prepare you'll get a faster start and this will increase your comprehension and confidence. If you prepare for your first day using the guidelines suggested here, you'll approach your first day organized and ready for your new job.

WHY PREPARE
FOR YOUR FIRST DAY?

Management will form their first opinion about you by how quickly you can get productive and how much you can accomplish. As a new employee you will be judged by how effectively (quickly and efficiently) you get your job done. That is reason enough to be organized in your personal life the day you step into your new job. It also makes good sense to organize your personal life so you can spend more time learning about your industry, your company, your department and your individual job.

You're in competition now for only a few available promotions. Your competition is with other grads, employees and new hires from outside your company. If you want to be promoted you must shine above the others. You'll be very busy and will wish you had organized your personal life if you have not done so. You have much information to absorb, learning what is required of you and assimilating information about others with whom you work. Additionally you'll be practicing skills and habits acquired from "Most Important Skill," "Good Work Habits" and "New Skills" (see chapters 2, 3, and 4 respectively). Managers will be looking to see who fits in well. If every day after work you're absorbed with apartment hunting or applying for phone, utilities, checking account, etc., you may miss important job opportunities. Preparation can equal promotion as Mike found out after he started his first job with an insurance company.

Mike decided to stay in his home town and party the week before relocating to Chicago instead of leaving early to find his apartment and to settle in. After all, he reasoned, he could stay with his uncle temporarily. Arriving Saturday night, he'd slept until noon, unpacked and was ready bright and early

Monday morning. He enjoyed the entire six-week employee training program which focused on product information and selling techniques. Required reading every night had left him no time to look for an apartment, but the company had been good about letting him off during the day to meet realtors. He'd met Mary, another grad who had been in his orientation class.

Mary had arrived three weeks before her start date. She had located an apartment, a roommate, and both utility and phone service. She had the entire training class laughing with her on a coffee break one afternoon as she described her escapades getting lost while driving to work before her first day. She drove to locate her way, to determine her commute time during rush hour, and to pick up a training manual in advance. She wanted to look it over before class.

After four weeks Mary asked to take the state insurance license exam early. She passed. Mike realized she was no smarter than he, but she had read the training manual before starting work and was able to make more sense out of the volumes of material they'd been given faster than he. Mike had a lot on his mind. Less than one year later Mary was promoted to a large account sales job and he wasn't even considered. Mike realized her fast start had given her a distinct advantage.

PREPARING YOUR PERSONAL LIFE

Mary had really given herself a head start when she determined to prepare and organize her personal life before her first day at work. Preparation for school and preparation for business are very different. You may have arrived at school the day before classes began and gotten away with it. That might not be the case with your new career.

Schools take good care of their students. They make dorms and fraternities available and have counselors to help students locate off-campus housing. In business you'll probably find there is no one to take care of your needs but you.

Are you thinking ahead? What are your housing goals? Will your needs best be served by getting an apartment or a house? Can you afford to buy, can you afford the time and responsibility it takes? Should you live by yourself or get a roommate? Would it be better if you lived close to work or farther away? Would the dollars saved in living in a less expensive neighborhood be worth the time and frustration commuters face? The following suggestions will help you make these decisions and save you frustrations, problems, time and money.

To help you organize, make a list of tasks necessary in preparing your personal life. What "lead time" will be necessary for each item? For instance, apartments often must be leased two to four weeks in advance, phone hookup and utilities requested one week to several days in advance. Checking and savings accounts can normally be opened immediately. Ask advice from a parent or another grad (at least a year or two ahead of you). Do those things first which require the longest lead time.

Apartment Or House?

Find a place you can live at least for one year before having to move. Get settled in before your first day of work; that means phone, utilities, furniture and kitchen supplies. Have your clothes cleaned and pressed for your first week. Don't be satisfied with temporary housing while you familiarize yourself with your new city; you need to get settled right away. What extra time you do have now you'll want to spend learning about your industry, your company and your job, not learning about the city. Save that for later.

Lease Or Buy?

Be conservative your first year; choosing expensive housing can be a major mistake. You probably won't qualify to buy; you probably won't want to buy. Your salary may sound big, but after taxes, pension, insurance and other deductions your take-home pay will be just over half what you thought it would be. Your expenses the first year will be higher than you anticipated because it will be necessary to purchase a number of items you've not needed before.

You'll need to buy appropriate clothing and accessories, you'll have cleaning and laundry expenses, lunches and transportation, not to mention your entertainment allowance. Socializing will be an important part of getting to know others and fitting in. A good rule of thumb is not to exceed 20% of your gross income for all housing-related expenses (rent, utilities, phone and maintenance). If you're moving a family your considerations will be different. But for our purposes we'll address issues related to the graduate only.

Roommate Or Solo?

There are many benefits to having a roommate. Most grads find they are so occupied with work-related activities they spend much less time than anticipated at their apartments the first year or two. You may have a desire to get out on your own and to live alone. Privacy may be very important to you. Use caution and prudence as you consider whether the money you'll spend on an apartment — which sits empty sixteen hours a day — will be worth the sacrifice you'll make in your paycheck. If you spend it on that vacant apartment you won't have it to spend on social activities or major purchases.

Sharing expenses on rent, utilities and phone is not the only benefit in having a roommate. A roommate can provide occasional companionship in a new city and can cover as much ground as you in locating needed services such as reputable mechanics, doctors, dentists, etc.

Most grads anticipate a very active social life their first year and want the privacy and luxury of solo living. They later learn that their social life starts slowly and usually takes a few months to establish. The first year will go by more quickly than you realize, with yet another decision about renewing your lease (and roommate commitment).

Remember to first put your energy and money into what's most important and that is your career. Stay conservative and frugal in your housing and personal life to allow yourself the luxury of putting all your energy and time into your career. It will pay off with faster promotions and higher earnings in the future.

Transportation

If you commute using mass transit, you may be able to get some office work done on the way to and from work. Try to maximize your available time learning about your job, company and industry. Know before your first day how you'll get to work, then make a practice commute. Yes, during rush hour! Check typically congested areas, accurate commute time, and your tolerance level for the transportation you've chosen. Adjust as necessary.

Arriving in Chicago Mary called a college friend, Sue, who worked nearby. "You've been here awhile, Sue, what do you think of my getting an apartment west of the office?" "It's great — if you don't mind not having any alternate transportation if something happens to your car — there's no train out there. Besides, you're driving into the sun every morning. Everyone I know who lives out there hates that part of it. You might be better off in one of the suburbs only fifteen minutes north of the office."

It was fortunate for Mary she had a friend to bounce ideas off of; she chose an apartment north that proved to be a good decision. She was ten minutes closer to work and took the train on bad days in the winter.

Vacation Prior To Start Date

Once you begin your new job you'll have much less time off than what you've experienced in school. The first six to twelve months on any new job are demanding. Take time off for a vacation, if you can, before your start date. Attempt to start work fully relaxed and totally rested.

Your company will have strict limitations on vacation time. As a new employee the length of vacation time you'll be allotted will seem very short compared to the breaks between semesters or quarters and the long summers many of us enjoyed throughout school. Typically, companies allow a maximum of two weeks vacation per year for the first three years. This can be a big adjustment for grads fresh out of school: especially when classes, lectures and labs had typically demanded less than eight hours a day. In business it's not unusual to clock eight to ten hours a day. Add to that an hour or two before or after work practicing your most important skill in formal or informal social opportunities. That makes for a long (but hopefully productive) day. The good news is that business is more fun than school. The long hours studying alone will be replaced by exciting interactions with enjoyable people all committed to achieving common goals.

RESEARCH YOUR COMPANY AND INDUSTRY

You'll be much more productive on your job — even the very first week — if you have an overview of your industry and company. Finding out about your company parallels your getting prepared in your personal life. Being organized from the beginning gives you a head start on the job you'll be required to do. So another very important part of being ready for your first day is to research your company.

You'll want to find out about the state of your industry, your company in general and your competitors in particular. Some companies can provide you with a great deal of information prior to your first day. Others will require you to be an active employee before they reveal much of anything. Some won't give what is considered "restricted information" even to their employees.

You'll want to find out exactly what your company does and how it makes its money. Who is president and CEO? When was your company begun and by whom? What is the past history of your company and what is its reputation for doing business? What are its strengths? Who are your competitors? Compared to other companies in the industry, what is the size of your company? What has been your company's track record and growth compared to competitors? What problems has your company experienced in the past? What difficulties does it face currently? What are its future challenges? What governmental regulations affect your company and industry? Do you have foreign competition? What is the strength of the foreign market in your industry? Find out what plans your company has for its future: its development, its growth.

Function And Purpose

What is the function of your company? Does it produce products or provide services? What parts of the product does your company produce, or what services does it provide? Does your company produce all of the product and service or does it refer parts to someone else, subcontracting out all, or part, of what you produce?

What product or service information can you find? Any product knowledge you have in advance of your first day on the job will prove invaluable to you. Not only will you appear informed, but you'll also be able to perform based on advanced understanding about the goals of your company. Can you find any product brochures or sales information? You'll fit in faster, sound more experienced and gain confidence in your ability if you obtain a solid base of information about your industry, company and job in advance of your first day.

LOCATIONS
Where and what kind of facilities does your company maintain? In what cities, states or countries do you have plants, offices, stores, service centers or sales reps?

EMPLOYEES
How many people does your company employ? How is your company organized regarding subsidiaries, parent companies, divisions, departments? How are employees grouped: work groups, product groups, geographic groups? A copy of your company's organizational chart will be the most helpful piece of information you can obtain at this point. It will give you the reporting relationships and job titles of all employees.

PROCEDURES AND BENEFITS

A valuable source of information can be found in both the rules and regulations and the systems and procedures your company uses to accomplish tasks and keep track of things.

Administration manuals, employee handbooks and training manuals are filled with information. However dull they may appear initially, they will provide valuable insights about how your company expects you to communicate with it and how it expects to communicate to you. These resource books also offer guidance in what's expected when, where why, and with whom.

Don't overlook benefit plans and medical information. Booklets will be available describing your company's insurance benefits, retirement program, plus savings and/or profit sharing plans.

SOURCES OF INFORMATION

There are a number of resources for obtaining this information about your company. The best source might be the person you dealt with during your interview process. Perhaps your company doesn't prepare a packet for new employees. In that case it may be your manager who will be able to help you the most.

Other sources for information include the public affairs department or stockholder information department, your company library, the local library or a good stockbroker. Don't overlook the valuable information you'll get from competitors and customers; how are these people treated by those within your company?

Returning to Mary, we know she had a head start because she'd done a little research on her own. After Mary had signed her lease and moved her belongings she treated herself to a "research day." She began in the morning spending two hours in the library looking up her company's history and comparing it to the top three competitors.   She found that their main competitor was a fairly new upstart which threatened only in its tremendous growth over the past five years.

After meeting her new roommate for lunch, she called three insurance agents and chatted briefly with them, identifying herself only as a potential client.   She also called one agent who she knew represented two of their competitors and asked for comparisons between the three companies.   She was careful to note the value placed on her competitor's product.

By the end of her "research day" Mary was confident that what she would be taught over the next six weeks would make much more sense than if she'd attended classes cold.

THE PAYOFF FOR BEING PREPARED

This research will pay off in the way you "appear" to have a better understanding of your work environment, a better ability to affect changes in the quality of work you perform, the positive attitude you employ and the relationships you enjoy.

One word of caution: don't try to impress anyone by what you think you know. What you do know, you'll later learn, is minuscule compared to what you'll later find out.   Do your homework in advance and remain alert to new information.

The day Mary's promotion was announced, Mike discussed reasons for the speed of her promotion with another grad. "The very first week we're riding up the elevator when this older guy comes in. I don't know who he is, although I've seen him. I go quiet. Mary calls him by name, comments on the proposed expansion in the new wing . . . . The next week the V.P. of

Marketing gives a talk during training and Mary asked which of our three major competitors presented the greatest threat to the new product just introduced? How did she know about the new product and that we had three major competitors; I thought we had only two. Of course, that set this marketing guy off for the next fifteen minutes. Don't you know he was impressed with her. Then just last week she interrupts me as we're walking down the hall to say 'hi' to a woman we'd met on our first day's tour: 'You're Glenna, Mr. Wilson's assistant, aren't you?' She was the Executive V.P.'s secretary — and even she was impressed! How did Mary remember her name? I barely even remembered meeting her. So I asked her and she says she's kept this organizational chart since the first day, along with a seating chart where she writes everyone's name and what they do. Wow, she really blew me away. She probably knows 50% of the people we pass. I probably know 10%. . . ."

What Grads Should Know:

WHY PREPARE FOR YOUR FIRST DAY?
   *Adequate preparation before you start work will
      give you more time to become productive faster
      and you'll be promoted sooner.

PREPARING YOUR PERSONAL LIFE
   *Have your personal life established before work
      starts, including housing, transportation and
      basic living needs. This will give you more time
      to concentrate on work. Be conservative in your
      choices of fixed expenses.

RESEARCH YOUR COMPANY AND INDUSTRY
*The more you know about your company and its
employees, products, customers and
competition, the faster you will fit into your
company.

Chapter 17

FIRST DAY

Quick Reference

- Company's Objectives
- What Happens the First Day
   New Employee Orientation
   Meeting with Your Manager
   Introductions to Employees
   Your Desk and a Tour
- Graduates' Objectives
- What Grads Should Know

This chapter will help you make the best impression on your first day. That's important. Your first day is the basis for many of your new co-workers' initial opinions of you. The preparation and knowledge you gain from this chapter will make their first impression the best it can be.

COMPANY'S OBJECTIVES

Your company's objectives the first day are threefold: 1) to provide you with basic information (as much as you can absorb) about the company, employees, procedures and work rules; 2) to continue the positive impression they have given you and to encourage a positive attitude on your part; and 3) to make you a productive employee as soon as it is possible.

WHAT HAPPENS THE FIRST DAY

To meet these objectives your company will employ one or more of several methods, either formal, informal or a combination of the two. You may spend the whole day with your new manager in informal discussions going over what is important for you to learn. Some companies provide group classes with other grads which are taught by a human resources person. Other companies may have you view videos and read employee instructional manuals, resource materials and handbooks. Some companies may put you on the job the very first day.

Be prepared for any or all of the above. Whatever approach is used, there are general rules that apply to your first day that will greatly enhance how you are seen by your peers and others within your company. It's important that you make a good impression because many of the people that you'll meet your first day may be very meaningful to you and your future success.

New Employee Orientation

Whether you attend a formal classroom or are in a less structured atmosphere, the new employee orientation is designed to give general company information to all new hires. The orientation should cover most of the following: general industry information, company and product information, company organization, work rules, employee information, benefits, forms and information about your job. An extensive employee orientation program can take more than one day. It may be broken up into parts of several days throughout your first week.

INDUSTRY AND COMPANY

The state of the industry provides you with increased understanding of the past problems, present difficulties and future challenges that your particular industry faces.

Information about your company's history — and plans for its future — will equip you to better understand the goals of management. Information about the products and/or services your company provides is integral for you to understand your job in relation to all other jobs within your company.

COMPANY ORGANIZATION

What should you know about your company that will help you to be more successful in your job? You should know how large your company is, where it is located, how many divisions or departments it has and how many people it employs. Here is the perfect opportunity to fill in any of the information from chapter 16, "Preparation for First Day." If you did your homework from that chapter it will pay off your first day. Your informed questions will earn respect and increase your capacity for understanding.

Now is the time to get out that organizational chart and fill it in as you meet others (see "Organization: Formal and Personal," chapter 8). Learn your job title and the job titles of others. Begin to get an overview of who reports to whom. This will provide clues later in the year when you are confused by a set of relationships or turn of events, such as an unexplainable promotion.

WORK RULES
Learn what is expected of you in terms of office hours, lunches and breaks. You might find this information in an employee handbook or administration manual. Understanding what is required will make your task of being efficient and cooperative that much easier. Be sure you know about access to your building, keys, ID badges, etc.

EMPLOYEE INFORMATION
You may be given an overview of job descriptions and the various departments and divisions within the company. Be prepared for required evaluations and exams (personality, drug or alcohol, and physical exams). You may be provided information about compensation, payroll and performance evaluations (format and frequency).

YOUR JOB
Learn about your job, your job title, job description and the duties you'll be given. You may be given additional training to perform your job in the work group, or groups, in which you belong (see Multi-Level Teams in "Team Duties" chapter 11).

BENEFIT PLANS
You'll be presented with information, and perhaps choices, about the types of benefit plans you prefer regarding health, disability and life insurance, and saving or pensions plans. Having thought about these in advance will make your choices easier. Read your company information carefully. Sign up for the plans best suited to your particular circumstances. Be prepared to complete a number of human resource records including enrollment forms, payroll forms, direct deposit forms

or other legal forms (work agreements, invention rules or competitor limitations).

Meeting With Your Manager

The purpose of the first meeting is for your boss to welcome you and to make you feel more comfortable. Grads sometimes don't realize the relationship with their manager is going to change. It will transform into a manager-employee relationship: from one of recruiting to one that is more business-like and structured. As an example, many managers do not answer telephone calls during employment interviews, but do answer calls during meetings with employees. Your manager may be interrupted many times during your first few meetings.

Your manager may do a great deal of your first day orientation, or he may delegate it. There's even a possibility he will be out of town your first week on the job. His job will come first, before your needs or your concerns. If you're prepared for this it will not surprise you.

Introductions To Employees

The faster you learn the names of the employees within your department and the duties they perform, the better equipped you'll be to do your own job. During the first day you'll have an opportunity to meet several people.   You'll be working closely with many of these same employees over the next few weeks, months and, perhaps, years. If it is possible to learn something about these people before you work with them, do so by getting hold of an organizational chart of the company and jot down the names and job titles of everyone you meet (refer to the chapter 8, "Organization: Formal and Personal"). If you don't have your company's organizational chart, at the very least construct a seating chart of employees' offices. Jot down employees' names and corresponding job titles (or duties).

Chance meetings sometimes happen and you don't have an opportunity to make notes. When you have an extra moment, write down the names of new acquaintances and what you've learned from them. The point is: learn the names of everyone and their job titles (or responsibilities) as quickly as you can. Don't hesitate to solicit another's help in learning the names and jobs of other employees.

THE RESPECTFUL ATTITUDE

One of the most important attributes you can possess is a respectful attitude. When you meet other employees be friendly, positive and respectful. Don't try to impress them with your education, knowledge or anything else. Listen attentively to what they say. Talk about — or ask questions about — subjects *they* bring up. You will do best in your company, and in your new job, if you realize you are the new kid on the block: the inexperienced one who has much to learn. Treat others with respect, not just sometimes, but always.

Mary's boss, Hank, offered to introduce the new grads to those they'd be working with their very first day. He was pleased by Mary's suggestion to see and make notes on an organizational chart before the introductions. He was further impressed as he noticed her concentrating on each person and being attentive to what they said, even though nearly every conversation was the same.

At lunch, afterward, Mary commented how surprised she was that all the introductions only took a minute or two each. Hank responded, "You made a very good first impression Mary. You were a pleasant surprise to several managers. They're used to grads trying to show how much they know and instead coming off as know-it-alls. You paid attention to what they were saying to you and didn't waste their time. They liked that."

DEVELOP GREETING SKILLS

Besides the respectful attitude, which may well be the cardinal greeting rule, there are other elements to the successful business greeting. They may be summarized as 1) shake hands, 2) give eye contact, 3) pronounce names, and 4) smile.

To shake hands with a firm handshake (neither feeble nor rugged) is important. Also, look people in the eye as you shake their hands; offering your hand readily to both men and women is equally important. Pronouncing their names as you indicate your interest or enthusiasm at meeting them confirms your acknowledgement. A smile lets others feel accepted and comfortable when they are around you; learn to smile easily.

Now relax, having practiced your greeting skills, and pay attention. Actively listen to what they have to say. Allow yourself to become absorbed in the conversation.

Your Desk And A Tour

YOUR DESK

Finally, home sweet home! It may not be much, but it's a place to do your work, to park your pens and to gather your thoughts. Be realistic about your accommodations. Don't imagine you'll get a big office with a view of the city. Be prepared when you're shown to your desk located in a cubicle at basement level.

Most companies have made reductions in the kind of office facilities they offer employees. There is less luxury and less privacy in work areas now than ten years ago. Fixed-wall offices are hard to adjust. When companies reorganize and it's

necessary to change walls, shoulder-high cubicles, which unbolt
and are easily movable, now add flexibility to the work space
and are more cost effective. Additionally, they allow for better
air circulation during months requiring heating or air condition-
ing.

What should you bring, or not bring, to your desk? Personal
items should be left at home. Photos, pictures, degrees and
desk accessories can be brought to your office during the second
or third week on the job. Some offices have strict rules about
what can be hung on the walls or displayed on your desk.
Personal items are very telling about who you are. Look around
and see what others have displayed in their cubicles or offices.
Determine from them what is appropriate.

TOUR OF OFFICE

You'll be given a tour of the physical facility to learn where
the lunchroom, bathrooms, plant, mail room and executive
offices are located. After you meet people jot down their names
and titles. Ask the person who gives you the tour who these
people are and what they do. Make additional notes when the
tour is over.

GRADUATE'S OBJECTIVES

Create a Good Impression

What are your objectives for your first day? We've discussed
your company's objectives for your first day, to: 1) provide
you with basic information, 2) continue the positive impression
they've given you, and 3) make you a productive employee as
soon as is possible. The two most important objectives you can
hope to achieve are to: 1) create a good first impression
(respectful, sociable and friendly) with everyone you meet, and

2) concentrate on getting to know other people and to learn what they do — learn how they fit into the organization.

For you to create a good first impression the following three aspects must be considered: 1) your business appearance, 2) your attitude, and 3) your personality. First, remember to dress for the part you play in creating the appropriate image for your company (see "Ideal Business Image," chapter 14).

Second, think carefully about your first day's attitude before your day begins. The key word that will generate the most goodwill is "respectful." Contrary to this, the most common "first day mistake" made by grads is the "know-it-all" attitude.

Third, and certainly not the least of these three impression-makers, is your personality. You will do well to act friendly, eager and happy. "First day talk" is introductory talk. It's just social small talk: "Welcome to the company. . . .   You'll like it here. . . . We sure can use some help around here. . . . Good to meet you. . . ." In this sort of brief greeting, your personality will be judged on your smile; nodding in understanding or agreement; and your positive, enthusiastic response in saying, "I'm very happy to be here," or "I can't wait to get started."

Concentrate On People

The most important thing you can do your first day is to concentrate on people and learn their names and responsibilities. Remember the adage that you were made with two ears and only one mouth; listen at least twice as much as you speak. Get to know who others are, who they report to and who reports to them.

The faster you get to know these people the faster you will be part of your new company and the sooner you will become a productive part of it. Greg really enjoyed his first day. He concentrated on addressing each person he met with enthusiasm, appropriateness and respect.

Before leaving for work, Greg looked in the mirror one last time, knowing that if he looked his best he could forget his looks and get on with the most important things about his first day: learning about others and absorbing as much information as he could. The drive was easy, he'd driven it yesterday so he wouldn't get lost. Arriving 15 minutes early, he stayed in the car and composed himself by glancing at the latest Sports Illustrated *and* USA Today. *He'd be armed with safe small talk: weather, sports and current events. He walked in exactly two minutes early.*

He walked to the receptionist's desk in the human resources department as prearranged. Seeing her name on the name plate, he offered her a smile, "Wanda, I'm Greg Stevens to see Jim Caplan. It's my first day." She noticeably relaxed at his friendliness and smiled back, "Welcome! I'll tell him you're here."

Greeting his recruiter was as easy as greeting Wanda. Greg had spoken with him three times before and had felt an immediate rapport. Being ushered into the room they would use for orientation, Greg met two of his coworkers. He was quick to introduce himself to them before that uncomfortable silence began to develop, "I'm Greg Stevens and this is my first day," he'd say, extending his hand first to Joan and then to Steve.

Four graduates would be going through new-hire orientation together. The morning was spent intermittently filling out forms, being given information for reading and resource, and listening to briefings and informative talks. Just before lunch all were directed to meet with their respective managers. Greg, Joan and Steve had all been assigned to Ben

Jones in the production division.   As Jim ushered them into Ben's office, Ben walked around his desk smiling broadly, "Sure am glad to see the three of you. We really need your help." Greg, being the closest, smiled and extended his hand, "Happy to be here, Ben, can't wait to get to work." He made sure he looked Ben Jones directly in the eye and shook his hand with just the right amount of firm pressure. He then listened, ready to absorb what Ben was to tell them all: "You'll have three days of orientation, three weeks of training and the rest focused on your job duties. Unfortunately the timing is unusual and I'll be on vacation for three weeks, so you'll report to Lloyd while I'm gone."   Greg was respectful and attentive, remembering to talk about what Ben found interesting.

After the two days of orientation and the day before Ben's vacation, Jim, Ben's counterpart in human resources — and a friend for years — stopped by Ben's office. "What do you think of your new hires, Ben?" Ben's smile widened, "I really like that Greg. He could be a good one; he's the best-prepared graduate we've hired in several years. He's done research on the industry and knows quite a bit about our products. I'm especially impressed with how he relates to everyone else. He's friendly, has a good sense of humor and seems to relate well to everyone from Wanda to our oldest. . . ." Jim seemed delighted by Ben's response. "What did they say about being crammed into the old meeting room?" Ben answered, "They were all pretty realistic. They seemed to understand they're starting out at the bottom; but they can't wait until the addition is completed, either. You did a good job in picking these three, Jim. None of them is a prima donna."

What Grads Should Know:

WHAT HAPPENS THE FIRST DAY
*New Employee Orientation - Your company may provide you with some or all of the information listed in the six sections to make you a productive employee as soon as possible.

*Meeting with Your Manager - Expect a subtle change from recruiter/candidate to manager/ employee

*Introduction to Employees - Remember you're new; show respect to all, don't be a "know-it-all."

*Your Desk and Tour - Expect your desk or cube to be modest; delay hanging personal items.

GRADUATE'S OBJECTIVES
*Create a Good First Impression - Use good greeting skills; be friendly and listen.

*Concentrate on the People - Learn names, jobs and reporting relationships.

COMMON MISTAKES TO AVOID
*Many grads try to impress new co-workers with how much they know and how smart they are, with the negative result of coming off as a "know-it-all."

*Many grads who aren't comfortable meeting new
  people don't concentrate on learning names, jobs
  and relationships.

———————

Chapter 18

SOLUTIONS TO 10 COMMON MISTAKES

QUICK REFERENCE

- Difference Between School and Business
- Most Important Skill
- Your Boss
- Organization
- Politics
- High Visibility Situations
- Team Duties
- Ideal Business Image
- Personal Life
- First Day

If grads know the most common mistakes and the solutions to avoid them they will be more successful in business. This chapter lists the ten most common mistakes graduates make. It gives the business reality of each mistake's misconception and a practical solution to avoid making each mistake.

1. DIFFERENCE BETWEEN SCHOOL AND BUSINESS

MISTAKE
Grads think their company's primary concern is to enhance their careers and help them succeed. They don't realize the change from a student's role as customer to their new business role as employee.

REALITY
In school grads pay to obtain an education. In business grads are being paid to serve customers and help the company make a profit. Their personal career progress is secondary to the work they're expected to accomplish.

SOLUTION
Concentrate on doing the best job and making any adjustments necessary. When given a chance, always take the "what is best for the company" point of view.

2. MOST IMPORTANT SKILL

MISTAKE
Grads assume that the same talents and skills they used in school will make them successful in business.

REALITY
In school success was achieved individually by studying, writing papers and taking tests. In business cooperating, motivating and influencing people using verbal skills will determine the grad's success.

SOLUTION
Concentrate on developing verbal skills and learn to develop positive relationships with all types of people. See "Most Important Skill," Chapter 2.

3. YOUR BOSS

MISTAKE
Grads don't realize the importance of their boss to their success in business.

REALITY
Your boss in business is equal to all your professors and all your grades combined.

SOLUTION
Learn what your boss wants. Concentrate on maintaining communications and demonstrating loyalty as described in "Your Boss," Chapter 6. Grads should adjust to their bosses' requirements.

4. ORGANIZATION

MISTAKE
Grads don't realize their careers can be harmed by employees with a low level of formal power but a very high level of personal power.

REALITY
The boss's secretary may be the second most powerful person in the office, based on personal power.

SOLUTION
Grads should learn about not only their company's formal organization, but how personal relationship create different personal power levels. Read "Organization: Formal and Personal," Chapter 8.

5. POLITICS

MISTAKE
Grads fail to realize a "positive relationship" attitude toward politics can benefit their careers; an "unfair advantage" attitude can harm them.

REALITY
In business there are many different attitudes toward politics. If grads develop a positive attitude they will be more successful.

SOLUTION
Learn to use the five political categories in "Politics," chapter 9, to predict employees' actions and benefit your career.

6. HIGH VISIBILITY SITUATIONS

MISTAKE
Grads fail to realize the importance of business social situations. They are judged by the same conservative, professional standards as during regular business hours.

REALITY
The grad's maturity and management potential is constantly being evaluated in lunches, hospitality suites and Christmas or retirement parties, especially by senior managers who don't have regular contact with grads.

SOLUTION
Grads should learn and practice the five rules for "social business conduct" listed in "High Visibility Situations," chapter 10, to make sure they present the proper image.

7. TEAM DUTIES

MISTAKE
Grads fail to realize they are part of a company-wide team whose goals may be different than the goals of their daily work-group team.

REALITY
Employees who identify with company-wide team goals of profitability and customer service are perceived as having greater management potential.

SOLUTION
Grads should learn to blend company-wide team goals with personal and work-group goals so that they identify with their company. Refer to "Team Duties," chapter 11.

8. IDEAL BUSINESS IMAGE

MISTAKE
Grads fail to understand the importance of a consistent, professional business image for their success.

REALITY
Grads are perceived as young, immature and inexperienced. A conservative, professional business image is more important to grads than it is to the older, more experienced employees.

SOLUTION
Grads should always tend toward the consistently formal, professional, conservative image as demonstrated by older, successful employees. See "Ideal Business Image," chapter 14.

9. PERSONAL LIFE

MISTAKE
Grads don't realize the average student's single, personal life may give them an unwanted reputation as a young, swinging single not ready for management responsibilities.

REALITY
Business employees are usually older, married and more conservative than most single grads. To fit the more mature, professional image grads should avoid the "swinging singles" stereotype.

SOLUTION
Grads should keep their personal life separate from business until they learn what is expected in their new company. Refer to "Personal Life," chapter 15.

10. FIRST DAY

MISTAKE
Grads don't realize their natural enthusiasm to show how much they know often comes off as a cocky-know-it-all to experienced employees.

REALITY
Every employee in the company knows more about the company, its products, customers and ways of doing business than the new grad does.

SOLUTION
Grads should start out with a respectful attitude: listen, learn and wait until they know what's going on before expressing ideas. See "First Day," chapter 17.

Emerson Taylor

Emerson Taylor has a B.A. in Labor Economics and a 25 year career in Human Resource Management. The first 19 years Taylor worked for two large, international corporations. The last six years of his career he has owned and managed a human resources consulting company providing services for all types of small businesses.

Taylor has hired, managed and observed the adjustments of graduates in companies from five to 20,000 employees. His various human resources job duties at one time or another have included all of the following:

College campus recruiting
Employee education and training
Career development
Hiring and performance evaluation seminars
Management evaluation and training
Labor negotiations and communications
Salary and compensation administration
Employee benefit management
Executive search and outplacement

Index